HOW TO GIVE THE ULTIMATE SALES PRESENTATION

The essential guide to selling
your products, services, and skills

by

Peter Kleyn and Josette Lesser

D1610418

This book is published by
Grosvenor House Publishing Ltd
28-30 High Street, Guildford, Surrey, GU1 3EL.
www.grosvenorhousepublishing.co.uk

A CIP record for this book
is available from the British Library

ISBN 978-1-78148-198-1

Contents

Acknowledgements

This book is very personal to us in both its layout and style. It is based upon our workshops, which have been very successful. We continue to run these for both large corporations and as external workshops for SMEs and individual entrepreneurs, both in Britain and abroad. We would like to thank all of those who have taken the time and trouble to provide us with such wonderful feedback. Many of these testimonials can be found on our website. We have enjoyed working with each and every one of you.

Of course, we could not have written this book without the wonderful work of many other authors and their insightful research. Please do look at our bibliography for further reading ideas.

And then there are those who have supported us throughout the process of writing this book. We would, therefore, like to thank Sally Kleyn, Martin Le Comte, Richard Wyeth, Edwina Hughes, and The Chartered Institute of Sales and Marketing Management.

Introduction

There is no doubt that selling, whether directly or indirectly, is a skill. You may be working as a salesperson selling products to individual customers, small companies, or even multinationals, or you could be selling a service or skill that may have nothing visible to demonstrate.

Or perhaps you are an entrepreneur with a new idea, a new product or a new service. However good the idea, you will still need to sell it.

On the other hand, you may not be formally selling at all – perhaps it is *you*, your skills or your knowledge that are your product? For example, you may work as an accountant, a copywriter, a dentist, a designer, a hairdresser, an IT specialist, a psychologist, a solicitor, a veterinarian . . . the list is endless – and you may indeed be freelance.

No matter what or how you are selling, there are times when you will need to sell yourself or your product, by delivering a presentation to one or more people – and however you dress it up, it is most likely going to be an integral part of your sales process. So integral that you could win or lose a sale or a contract based on this part of the process alone. Every presentation to a potential customer or client is, in fact, a *sales presentation*.

At this point, it is also important that we mention another form of sales presentation, and that is the presentation given during a bidding process. Bidding is becoming more and more common when selling your goods and services to larger organisations, particularly to the public sector. This begins with putting in a written tender, which is used to draw up a shortlist of potential suppliers. If you are selected, there is a good chance that you may then be asked to present a bid defence – in layman's terms, a sales presentation.

Everything we cover in this book, from the suggestions and recommendations on delivery to answering questions and closing, are as relevant in the bidding process as they are in any 'normal' sales presentation. And, as in all presentations, we have to emphasise the importance of getting your planning and preparation right.

But what are the best ways of ensuring a successful sales presentation? What are the components that allow you to excel at this stage? How can you best engage your audience? What should you be saying and doing for greatest impact? How do you demonstrate your product to best effect? If you have nothing to physically demonstrate, what evidence can you provide to show the credibility of your service? What can you do to move your sale forward? Can you close a sale at the end of your presentation? What is the most effective way to achieve that sale?

This book will not only answer these questions and many others, it will also provide you with a set of skills that can be utilised in many different aspects of your working life.

The book is set out in what we would perceive to be the order that you yourself would construct and deliver your sales presentation. We start with the actual planning involved and finish with your presentation close, before we hand over to you to work your newfound magic!

What follows is a mixture of tried and tested examples and styles, along with some of the latest research and techniques, and our own professional experiences and learning – all of which can help you to sell your products, services or skills. We have also tried to lighten the delivery of the information. Certainly we have had fun writing this book, and we make no apologies for the quips and asides contained herein.

You will also find worksheets at the end of this book. We recommend that you complete these as you go along and then refer to them before conducting your sales presentation. We also suggest that you revisit your answers once you have actually carried out your presentation. Would you answer them differently? Would you tweak or add any information?

CHAPTER 1

Planning your Pitch
and your Presentation

Researching who and what you're up against

Planning for a successful presentation is as important as the presentation itself – and key to this is knowing the audience you will be facing.

Unfortunately, it is a fact of business life that many of the sales presentations you give will be to a pre-selected audience. You may, for example, be asked by a company to deliver your pitch to specific representatives.

This is particularly true in a bidding process, where you may well be up against three or four other prospective suppliers. In this situation, you will most likely be presenting to representatives of the purchasing organisation.

Where you have no influence over who is attending, it is vital to ask the buyers who they have selected to be present. A lot of people feel that they can't ask this, but you will be pleasantly surprised to know that they will usually be quite forthcoming about this. We will talk more about the types of people who might attend later on, but the answer you are given is a clue to how hard you can push for a close at the end of your presentation.

It is also important to establish on what basis the decision to buy will be made. Examples of this include price, ability to deliver to an agreed timescale, or the necessity to meet a technical requirement. This might be hard to come by, particularly when dealing with the public sector - sometimes buyers will be happy to tell you and sometimes they won't. If you can find out these factors, it goes without saying that they should be highlighted in your presentation and in your close. The fact that you are showing this knowledge also holds great sway with the buyers.

You may also wish to find out the strengths and weaknesses of your competitors – particularly in a bidding presentation. If you can find out who they are, research them thoroughly – particularly any new products or services that you may find you are competing against. Then search for articles and feedback. You may find a chink in their armour. You can then use this information to highlight your relative strengths and promote the unique selling points (USP) of your own product or service. (But don't run your competitors down.)

If you can't find out who your competitors are, why not ask the buyers who they currently use?

If you still draw a blank, then just make sure you have really studied your market sector. Let's face it – any good salesperson should know who their main competitors are, and their strengths and weaknesses.

Who to invite to your presentation

We have spoken about knowing your audience and the times when you won't be able to influence who is there. However, there are times when you *are* able to have some input as to who will attend. In fact, it is in your best interest to request certain people be present - after all, you are there to make a sale, and you need to progress or even close that sale as promptly as possible. So always ask if you can have the option of requesting that certain people attend.

You may already have a good idea about the company or organisation you are going to see, but what you think you know, or what you knew about them six months or a year ago, may not hold true now. Is that rumour of an acquisition true? Have any of the key players changed? Is there a biography of your audience members online? All of this will help you to make your presentation relevant to your potential client.

If you are doing an external presentation, possibly to different organisations or companies, do they complement one another and have common areas of interest, or are they more diverse, with differing needs?

Your content will vary considerably depending upon your answers to these questions. Having the right audience sets the tone and the speed with which you can make a sale. The question is: who is the right audience?

The key players

For a sale to be made, your ideal audience needs to consist of a number of key people.

In fact, there are potentially *five* roles that can influence this process and who, ideally, should be represented in your audience:

- Decision maker
- Influencer
- User/s
- Advisor/Expert
- Ultimate authority

The Decision Maker

Of greatest importance is the decision maker or makers. These may be specific individuals, or individuals who hold a specific

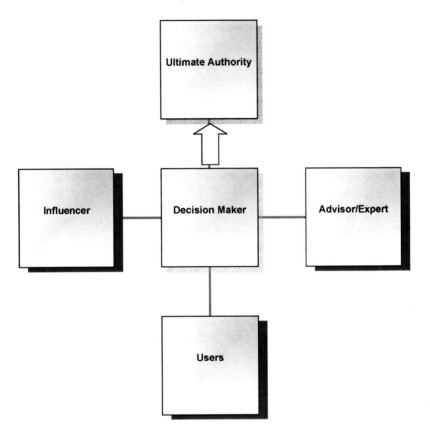

role. One tried and tested method of qualifying someone's ability to buy is to use the acronym MAN:

- **M**eans
- **A**uthority
- **N**eed

The decision maker should be part of your audience and demonstrate all three of these traits.

The *means* is simply having the finances or resources to pay. However, you need to establish that there is actually a budget in place - or at least a plan to create a budget. If there is no budget, what is the likelihood of your audience be able to afford your product or service?

The *authority* is sometimes harder to define, and differs from organisation to organisation. If, as we have discussed, they have an approved budget, then the decision maker should have authority over that budget. If there isn't a budget, the decision maker must at least have the authority to proceed, and be able to seek financial approval. It is important to clarify these issues early on.

For you to be able to sell your product or service, an organisation must have a *need*. Of course, they may not recognise this, so creating that need is up to you. They may have a 'want', but let us be honest a 'want' is only an aspiration, whilst a *need* is an essential. (We both *want* the latest Porsche, but what we *need* is a car that goes from A to B.) Many people may want what you supply, but that will not necessarily get you a sale. So creating a need for the decision maker is vital.

Sometimes you will have to uncover that need, and a decision maker may often have his or her own agenda, of which you should be aware. Never be afraid to ask questions ahead of your presentation. It may well help to understand their points of view and even their motivation.

A lot of this is about understanding and building relationships with your prospects and clients. As the sales profession has progressed, people skills have become more and more important. These can be learned, and there are communication techniques, many grounded in psychology, that can be used to assess motivational factors in these situations. We will come back to those later.

Even when the primary decision maker is at your presentation, in many cases, there will probably be others who have a role in the decision-making process. This is one of the major benefits of giving a group sales presentation, rather than simply having a one-to-one meeting with the decision maker.

The Influencer

The influencer can also play an important role. One example of an influencer is a financial director, who may not make decisions directly, but does have influence over how the product or service is paid for.

A company may also have a procurement department. Their only interest will be in pricing and profit – in other words, getting the best deal – and any influence they exert will be based on number crunching, rather than on your product or service.

Other directors or managers may also play a similar role because their individual departments might be affected. For example, whilst a Managing Director may make the decision to buy new computer equipment, it would be important for them to involve the IT Manager at an early stage of the decision-making process.

The Users

Users may not necessarily have the authority to make a buying decision, but they have influence and can provide obstacles or support in the decision-making process. They will want to know how much your product or service will affect them, including the amount of training required and the level of support they can expect once your product or service has been purchased. Think of a secretary being asked to use new software, for example.

It is always worth checking whether a user is in your audience before you arrive. This will allow you to prepare for any more specific questions that may arise. Getting user buy-in is important, and you should think about angling your presentation accordingly. Perhaps it needs to be more technical? Or perhaps you need to make the whole presentation more features-orientated? The key message here is: adapt to your audience.

There may even be times when you find yourself presenting solely to end users. In this case, you have to accept that there will be no final decision made at this point.

The Advisor/Expert

The main influencer may bring in an advisor or expert within the area of your product or service as part of the decision-making process. There may well be someone within the organisation who is considered a real expert - whether they are or not! However you perceive their ability, this person may well carry some influence with the decision maker, simply because they have a good reputation within the company. In some cases, organisations may turn to external advisors such as buying consultants and support professionals.

However, do note that the decision maker may often listen to these people enthusiastically, and then override them.

The Ultimate Authority

Lastly, whilst you may have established that the decision-maker can give you the go-ahead, there may still be an 'Ultimate Authority' who will need to ratify that decision. This is particularly relevant when dealing with some overseas organisations where the culture is very much one of 'team approval'. Scandinavia is a prime example. There, this ultimate authority may take the form of a Board of Directors, a more senior manager, the CEO, or the Managing Director. In fact, it can often be in the decision maker's own interest to invite someone along who has the authority (potential or otherwise) to overturn their decision, simply to expedite matters.

PETER: *I certainly experienced this in my early years in France, where I was told by the Patron [the equivalent of a CEO] that a specific person was the decision maker, and to present to him. However, after I had made my pitch and won over this decision maker, the Patron then decided against the deal and simply overruled him.*

It's clear that for the best results, it is important that more than one person is present at your sales presentation. The question is then, how many of the above people should actually be there?

The real answer is dependent on each individual situation. As a minimum, the decision makers and at least the main influencers should be present. The remainder is down to what is practical. If you don't know which people represent the roles above, just ask! Otherwise, you risk presenting to the wrong people or worse still, having to do the whole thing over again. In both cases, you have wasted your time and theirs.

But what if my hands really are tied, we hear you cry? What if I have no say whatsoever as to who will be there? Well, this is a possibility, but that does not stop you from asking your main contact what part those people attending will play in the decision-making process.

EXERCISE

Use Worksheets 1a: Analysing your Audience & 1b: Inviting an Audience.

In Worksheet 1a, fill in the name and title of the person fulfilling each role and whether they will be attending e.g. John Smith, Technical Director. Yes.

Given the opportunity, who else would you like to invite and why? Complete Worksheet 1b.

Clarifying your goals

Before giving a presentation of any kind, there are two questions you really should ask yourself: "Why am I doing this?" and "What exactly do I want to achieve?" In other words: what is the goal of giving this presentation?

Of course, your main aim is most likely to be to get the sale, progress a sale, or even establish a statement of intent. Another way of looking at this is to think about your presentation in terms of informing, persuading, proving and achieving.

But there are other benefits to a sales presentation that you should consider. These include promoting or launching a new product, establishing or re-establishing the credibility of your company (and, to some extent, your own credibility), showing off the infrastructure that supports your product or service, building rapport with a new customer, or reinforcing an existing relationship.

EXERCISE

Use Worksheet 2: Meeting your Sales Presentation Goals

Consider why you are giving your sales presentation: What are your goals? Use the worksheet to define your goals and objectives.

Then, in the table at the end of the worksheet, record the resources and actions required to achieve these goals or objectives.

Whatever the objective of your presentation, it is important that your goals are clear in your own mind, realistic and, most importantly, not forgotten. It is all too easy to give a good presentation, sit down to congratulatory comments, and not achieve your goal.

Objective versus Message

As we have discussed, the objective for your presentation is most likely to be to get a sale, progress a sale, or at least establish a statement of intent. But your presentation should also make a point. This point is your message, and there may be more than one. These are often referred to as key messages, and in a sales environment they are, quite simply, the benefits of your product or service.

It is a harsh lesson, but prospects (prospective buyers) buy the benefits and not the features or advantages of your product or service.

But what do we mean by features, advantages and benefits?

Features are probably the most obvious. These could include how a product looks, what it does, how it does it, and even the price. For services, this could be about what you do, how you do it, and how you deliver what you do.

Advantages are the improvements that these features bring to a client. This could be the end results, ease of use, or performing better than a competitor.

Benefits can sometimes be harder to pinpoint. An excellent acronym for recognising benefits is SIS:

- **S**ave
- **I**ncrease
- **S**olve

Does your product *save* time or money, *increase* effectiveness or production, and *solve* a problem no other product or service can solve? If so, then it is important to get these points across to your audience.

For example, if you have a service to sell, such as insurance, the *features* are that it is inexpensive, gives great cover, and can be applied for online. The *advantages* are that it is cheaper than your competitor, the cover is more comprehensive, and it is easy to apply for. However, it is the *benefits* that these *features* and *advantages* provide that the prospect is actually buying: *saving* time and money, *increasing* a client's sense of security, and *solving* the problem of out-of-hours access.

There is a simple way of testing whether what you are actually offering is a benefit (rather than a feature or advantage). It is called the "So what" test. Look at the following examples:

1. *This photocopier produces 50 copies per minute.*

   "So what?" That is a feature, not a benefit.

2. *This photocopier is quicker than its competitors.*

   "So what?" That is an advantage, not a benefit.

3. *It will run continuously.*

   "So what?"

You get the idea?

The potential messages/benefits in these examples are that the person buying the photocopier *saves* time, *increases* productivity, and *solves* the problem of overtime.

EXERCISE

Use Worksheets 3a & 3b: Feature, Advantage, Benefit

Look at the completed example for a photocopier on sheet 3a. This should provide you with some ideas for your own product, service or skills.

Now, take one of your own products, services or skills and use Worksheet 3b to list the five main features in Column 1. Then list an associated advantage of each feature in Column 2, and finally, list a benefit of that feature in Column 3.

If you are faltering with the benefits, a simple guide is to test what you have written with "So what?"

International presentations

As well as the team decision-making ethos in some countries, which we discussed earlier, it is important to consider the cultural differences between your own country and the countries with which you are dealing.

In some countries, the most important person may enter the room last, whilst in others, he or she will lead their team in to your presentation. For example, in some Latin countries the CEO would be expected to enter first. However, in some eastern European countries - particularly in a larger company, a senior executive may exercise their authority by deliberately holding back and keeping everyone waiting.

Far Eastern culture revolves around respect and extreme formality. It is important to acknowledge all participants in the buying process and also to recognise the formalities when presenting oneself, as well as the product or service you are selling. Whilst there are some slight differences in the various countries of the Far East, this aspect remains constant. And do not expect quick sales until you have developed their trust.

In Germany, there are also certain rules that are useful to know. It is quite common for senior staff to bring along more junior staff to a sales presentation, even if they are not involved in the decision to buy. Hence, it is even more important to understand who the key personnel are. Make sure nobody feels left out and make contact with everyone in the audience. You need to know if the purchasing department is represented. If not, remember not to bypass them in the sales process. Their involvement is simply one of the German 'rules'. Furthermore, it is wise to appear formal before, during and after a presentation.

What about your language? Are you using appropriate salutations? In the western world, we think it is fine to call someone we have just met by their first name. In other countries, this would be the height of rudeness.

Are your gestures and body language appropriate? A simple hand gesture in Britain can be completely misconstrued in some other cultures.

And a warning here: just because you think you speak the same language does not mean you do. George Bernard Shaw is attributed with having said that: "Britain and America are two countries divided by a single language." There seems to be no written record of this, but certainly in *The Canterville Ghost*, Oscar Wilde wrote: "We have really everything in common with America nowadays except, of course, language." Whoever you wish to credit for the sentiment, it is so true, and misuse of a common word in one language can have a shattering impact.

One case in point is the parliamentary term 'to table a motion'. In Britain, that means you are putting a proposal forward. In the US, you are setting it aside!

And finally, have you packed appropriate attire? Women in particular should be aware of cultural taboos such as baring shoulders, or showing too much skin. On the other hand, more formal countries would expect every man to wear a tie.

Our advice is, if you are going abroad, always do your research into your hosts' customs and practices.

CHAPTER 2

Preparing for Greater Success

There has been much written about whether or not a presentation should be standardised. The majority of publications argue that standardisation produces better results by a long way. You may think that your prospects are all different but, as we have discussed, prospects and potential buyers all buy for the same reasons: the benefits.

Top sales people in any industry will tell you that a standardised sales presentation delivered many times will produce the best results. Not only can you practise and deliver a standard presentation, but standardised themes hit home best with an audience.

PETER: *One of the most successful saleswomen I know uses the same formula in both her presentations and conversations when selling her piano business. She has standardised these to such a degree that she is able to deliver her patter with the greatest of ease and informality. The result is that she produces staggering sales results.*

However, standardisation does not mean inflexibility. The key here is relevance.

It is important to standardise the main content or core of your presentation and keep your key messages strong and well rehearsed. But you must also adapt to the requirements of each potential customer, and those benefits and advantages may well vary depending on their needs. In fact, you may actually wish to develop a couple of different standardised presentations to allow for different types of customers - perhaps corporate versus small business, for example. You can reuse these with other similar prospects in the future.

We liken it to a CV. You would not send out the same CV to every job you apply for. Instead, you would look at the specific requirements of the work and the company. Hopefully, you would then tweak some of the information you provide to best fit that job or organisation. It's the same with a sales presentation. If you know that a company values certain aspects more than others – for example, delivery time over cost per unit, then re-evaluate your basic presentation to highlight this. Add or subtract a slide if you are doing a PowerPoint, and adjust any demonstrations or proving accordingly. And do not do this on the hoof. Practise what you want to say, as you would with your main presentation.

A good sales presentation is never wasted. A successful sales presentation can be used again and again.

Even if a sale is not made at the time, if a commitment to proceed has been secured, it has been worthwhile. Some of the best salespeople would probably only admit to closing a sale on 50% of their presentations, but they have imparted their key points and progressed a sale to the next stage.

Appropriate presentation lengths

When it comes to the length of a presentation, your immediate reaction might be that the longer the presentation, the more you can fit in. This may work well in principle but, in reality, it is better to make your points and stop than to continue for too long and lose your audience. Much will depend on the audience you have, your products or services, how long it takes to demonstrate or prove these and, of course, how much time has been allocated to you.

Research has shown that most adults will maintain attention for just 20 minutes, after which their level of interest will wane.

So, if your customer hasn't stated how long they would like your presentation to run, we would suggest 20 minutes is probably an excellent length. Q&As can be additional to this, as they are, in themselves, stimulating. If your prospect is interested in your product or service, they will wish to ask you questions.

How to shape your presentation

Believe it or not, the *shape* of your presentation is as important as its content. Your sales presentation is a vital step in the sales cycle, and therefore it is important to construct your presentation so that it behaves like any other part of the sales process. This means clearly communicating your relevant points - your features, advantages and benefits – whilst moving the sale forward. To do this, your presentation needs to have a logical and progressive structure. Think of your presentation as a story. It should be well crafted for the greatest impact. In other words, it requires a beginning, a middle, and an end.

The Beginning

People buy from people they like, and we will discuss first impressions later in the book. But for those who have ever heard that they should start with a joke, because "that'll get 'em on your side", please don't! It may work for the Best Man at a wedding, and you might get away with it if you have met your audience before and have built sufficient rapport with them. Building rapport and relating to your audience is very important, but jokes in a cold sales environment can simply undermine your credibility.

It is also important to grab your audience's attention from the start, so try not to be too predictable. If you begin with, "Thank you for your time, I know how busy you all are, blah blah . . .", well they have already stopped listening. Plus, you are stating the obvious.

The beginning of your sales presentation is your introduction. It is about whetting your audience's appetite, introducing yourself, your company or your service, and tempting them with an insight into the benefits you are going to highlight in the body of your presentation - in other words, signposting that you will prove why they will want to buy from you.

In the words of Dale Carnegie (author of *How to Win Friends and Influence People*): "Tell the audience what you're going to say, say it; then tell them what you've said." Or as Paul White, the first Director of CBS radio news, put it: "Tell them what you're going to tell them. Tell them. And then . . . tell them what you told them."

So, in your introduction, you will tell the audience what you're going to say in the main body of your presentation. You will go into detail in this middle section. And at the end, you will recap what you've said.

This is particularly true in a bid situation, where it's imperative for you to explain why you are there as a bidder, and outlining what you have to offer. In this way, you are confirming to them that you have understood the tender, as well as being able to offer them exactly what they have asked for.

In a general presentation, you would also direct the audience as to when you will take questions – whether it's as you go along or at the end of your presentation. There are pros and cons to both. Taking questions as you go along can derail you, which is why most people take questions at the end. However, this is a sales presentation, so it is best not to be too prescriptive and simply remain flexible.

Different people have different styles, but whatever your style, initial buy-in from your audience is very important. So getting them involved and engaged is a priority.

Here are three examples of strong openers:

1. The Rhetorical Question

    Peter likes to start with a rhetorical question to which a prospect has to say, or at least think: "Yes." He then proceeds to tell them about a major benefit associated with this. This is followed by a brief introduction and something that will make them want to hear more.

PETER: *As an example, I might say: "Would you like to make more sales?" Then, after a brief pause, I'll add, "Yes, I thought so. Well, our 'How to Exceed in Sales . . . Delivering the Ultimate Sales Presentation' one-day workshop is designed to help you achieve outstanding sales results. My name is Peter Kleyn, and I'm here to tell you how the workshop will . . ."*

Rhetorical questions are usually what are termed "closed" questions. That means they will only elicit a "yes" or "no" answer. These sorts of questions normally start with:

"Do you . . .?"

"Have you . . .?"

"Would you . . .?"

"Are you . . .?" etc.

You can find out more about rhetorical questions in Chapter 3.

A similar technique to this is to ask your audience to think about something positive that would result from using your product or service. This works by using phrases such as: "Imagine how impressive your brochures would look if you used a more professional software." Or: "Think about how many more sales you would make by designing more professional brochures." And then, as with a rhetorical question, you would proceed into a key benefit.

2. The Fatal Alternative

The Fatal Alternative starts with a negative proposition. Here, someone immediately points out what could happen if you *didn't* buy their product or service.

PETER: *A classic example I heard recently was an IT security sales professional who started his presentation with a scenario that showed a company losing all of its data, and the devastating impact that it had on them.*

3. Second Place

The Second Place approach involves talking about a prospect's greatest competitor, and how that competitor is superior in some way. You would then demonstrate how if this company purchased your product or service, the situation would be reversed, and they would be in the superior position. This works very well in a competitive market.

For example: "I have just had a meeting with X [a very well known competitor], and their sales have gone through the roof using our product/service."

There are no strict rules as far as the length of your introduction is concerned. We have heard people quoting 10% of the total time allocated. Your beginning is simply a lead into the main event (the middle), so you may find that it is quite brief - only a few minutes, and there is no harm in this. Just make sure that you have signposted what is to come.

The Middle

We have said that your presentation should make a point or points, and that these points are your key messages. The middle is the main body of your presentation, and it is here that you should develop the expectation and interest you have created in your introduction. It is important that you provide greater insight into your key messages - the features, advantages, and most importantly, your benefits.

It is also worth including helpful references, and a list of customers – particularly those with whom your audience can identify, plus testimonials where possible.

You should also find examples that validate your product, service or skill: stories, third-party endorsements, anecdotal evidence, statistics, or even visual proof, such as a supporting video. Then, as with everything else, deliver these with a beginning, middle and an end.

A quick word of warning, if you are going to quote statistics for your product or service versus those of a competitor - make sure you double-check them and also give references. This is particularly relevant in a bid presentation. Don't forget your competitor may well be quoting conflicting figures. Giving references to support your figures will always count in your favour.

JOSETTE & PETER: *We always laugh at the old saying: "There are three types of lies: lies, damned lies, and statistics". It's attributed to Benjamin Disraeli, but the upshot is that you can make statistics say anything. For example, saying that 49% of people are against politician X, sounds convincing until you present it the other way around . . . 51% of people support politician X! Say it with aplomb; provide supporting evidence and your audience will go with the strongest argument.*

Whatever you include though, we cannot stress enough that this all needs to be clear, concise, comprehensible, relevant, and *interesting*!

In addition, it is wise to try to head off any inevitable questions or objections that might arise. For example, if you are commonly asked how your product is implemented, include this in the body of your presentation (and, of course, explain the benefits). Or, if people always complain that your delivery time is slow, pre-empt this with a positive statement, such as that each product is individually crafted for their specific needs.

Be careful with this approach, though - one enthusiastic sales person we know was so keen to pre-empt every possible objec-tion that his presentation lost total focus – and the interest of his audience. By all means prepare for every eventuality, but aim to include those points that are relevant to each particular audience.

Things to avoid

Certain industries are famous for jargon, but do avoid it wherever possible. It can cause misunderstandings or make your point unclear.

Do not assume that the audience understands your product in its entirety. It never hurts to restate the obvious – it may only be obvious to you.

Avoid waffle. The points you make must be clear, relevant, and accessible, not buried in long, involved explanations. And don't stray off topic – you will lose impact and confuse your audience.

Avoid leaving points unfinished. Not finishing succinctly can weaken your key message or messages. Give them a beginning, a middle, and an end.

Avoid reams of facts and figures. Unless that is what your presentation is about (although we cannot imagine why it would be), give overall figures, laid out clearly, to show benefits. If someone wants to know more, they'll ask.

Avoid acronyms – or at least explain them, so that everyone knows that you are all speaking about the same thing.

JOSETTE: *In Britain, TA is the short form for the Territorial Army, but to a psychologist TA refers to Transactional Analysis.*

Avoid criticising your competitors. By all means, mention how you supersede them, if and only if you have researched the facts and can back them up, but never run down or talk negatively about them or their products. Not only does it appear unprofessional, but you are opening yourself up to an argument.

The End

So we have a beginning, a middle, and now we must look at how to end your presentation.

This is your summary and, because this is a sales presentation, also your close.

So what goes into your summary? Quite simply, it is a brief overview of the key points you have made in your main/middle section – in this case, your benefits. Once you have done this, it may then be the right time to go in with your close.

When you are planning your close, consider what you would like the audience to do after the presentation.

We will cover different types of closes later, but as an example, if you want your audience to make a decision there and then, make sure that you have everything you need to actually make that sale.

If you want a follow-up meeting, have your diary ready and be clear about who needs to be present. Also, clarify the objective or objectives of that next meeting. It is no good having a meeting just for the sake of it.

> ## EXERCISE
>
> *Use Worksheet 4: Shaping your Sales Presentation*
>
> Your sales presentation must have a beginning (intro), middle (body of content), and end (summary and close).
>
> Complete the Worksheet with the key content for each section of your presentation

Preparing your visuals

Some research suggests that 80% of learners take in information visually. It is, therefore, reasonable to suggest that providing visual input will enhance your presentation's impact on the largest majority of people.

Nowadays, most visuals tend to be electronic, although never dismiss the fact that a flipchart can seem more low key and friendlier – and there are times when that is a bonus. For example, if your sales presentation includes any aspect of training, writing on a flipchart can be less intimidating, more inclusive, and seem more interactive. It also seems to encourage the audience to chat to you as you present – a tool that can be very useful for rapport building. So low-key does not necessarily mean low-impact. Plus, the lighting is natural, which allows for better eye contact with your audience.

But for most people, PowerPoint will be the way to go. So the first thing to consider is whether you are doing a *PowerPoint presentation* or whether you are doing a *presentation using PowerPoint*.

In a PowerPoint presentation, PowerPoint itself is dominant and the presenter is just there to flick through the slides. This is about letting the slides speak for themselves. However, working in this way steals focus from a presenter and doesn't allow them to have rapport with their audience. Even more importantly, a slide can't close a sale. You as a sales person need to interact with your audience to do that.

A presentation using PowerPoint means that the slides are there to *aid* the presenter, and offer visual corroboration. This can be an excellent sales tool.

If used properly, PowerPoint will support your sale and help you to look polished and professional. To do this, your slides must be engaging, content must be short and to the point, and each slide should follow a consistent format. Graphics, videos and photos must be sharp and of high quality, graphs or figures must be simple to read and clear, and any corporate logos really should be accurately depicted – this is a great opportunity to promote your company.

Your slides should build to your call to action, i.e. what you want the prospect to do after the presentation (more about that later.) And do include contact details – names, e-mail addresses, phone number, and address . . . whatever is relevant.

So, what about the content? A PowerPoint presentation should be like any mailing or marketing campaign; however great it looks, it is the *content* that will sell your product or service.

One fatal mistake many presenters make is writing out their whole presentation onto a slide. If you do this, it will have two major effects: firstly, you will find yourself using it as a crutch and reading from it, whether you intended to or not. Secondly, and perhaps more importantly, you will lose the interest of your audience, who are likely to stop listening to concentrate on reading what you have written on your slide.

The key here is to use bullet points. Our mantra is: "Less is more". Slides need to be clear, uncluttered, and relevant, and a bullet point is just that – a couple of focused words or a succinct phrase, not a full sentence.

The words you choose should be the ones that are most important to your pitch. So writing: "This has 42 widgets" is less punchy than making a bullet point that says: "42 widgets". In the same way, writing: "This was discovered to be the most powerful product in the world", will not stand out as much as just saying: "The Most Powerful Product in the World".

So, how many bullet points on a slide? In some countries, presenters use the 8 x 8 rule, which suggests no more than eight lines per slide, and no more than eight words per line. For us, that is far too many.

Four or five lines are optimum - six at most. But any more than six is a step too far. Our advice is the 5 x 5 rule. Plus, you don't need a slide for everything you are saying.

And one final plea - please spell check your slides, and then visually check them. Some typos may be correctly spelled, but might be the wrong word. For instance, omitting an 'r' so that you have "fist" when you meant "first".

We would also like to make a quick point about animation. By all means fly in a heading or reveal your key points for impact - but too much or continuous action is a distraction.

Your next consideration is choosing the colour of your wording, and the background colour of your slides.

The look of a slide is quite subjective, but as a rule, it's best to keep the colours fresh and clean, and keep your font style simple and consistent. Too much colour on a slide is distracting and can make it hard to read. Black or dark blue font is easy on the eye, particularly on a white background.

This also works in reverse. A colourful, tastefully placed flash or logo on a slide can look great, but bright or clashing colours for any other reason really are a no-no. Your company logo may be yellow and green, but writing with yellow font on a green background will not work. It is also worth remembering that, if you have a large audience, the chances are that someone will be colour-blind or has problems with colour recognition. Colour used cleverly can enhance. Colour used badly can make things harder to read.

You will be able to find books and online information on using colours effectively, but if in doubt, stand back from your screen and look for yourself. Can you read everything without straining – and without feeling sick?!

Of course, we all know that "a picture paints a thousand words", and a picture, chart or diagram can be extremely impactful and engaging. But it has to be relevant. A cute dog gnawing at a bone to show your company's tenacity may get a reaction (and yes, we have seen this done), but if there is also writing on that slide, we guarantee that no one will read it. Certainly, have a picture or an illustration, but consider: is it relevant? Does it portray the image you want to get across? (A cute dog does not say corporate to us, even if it alludes to tenacity.) Is there something better you could have had on that slide?

Using videos in a PowerPoint presentation can be very effective. Videoed testimonials are an excellent use of this medium, as are filmed demonstrations that cannot be done in situ. But the same rules apply as with any other slide or illustration - they need to be used for a reason, relevant to what you want to get over, relatively short and, as with your photos, of good quality when it comes to production and playback. That includes the sound, as well as the picture.

If you are imparting information or statistics in the form of a chart or diagram, we would always recommend you show the bottom line and explain how you got there. Anything too complicated will either lose your audience or distract them. If the audience is trying to decipher your slide, they are not listening to the point you are making.

By all means, show the explanations, but red lines crossing blue lines with green lines showing x and orange lines showing y, with two graphs superimposed to show this year's figures against last year's . . . well, you get the gist. As we've already said, if people want more in-depth figures or information, they will ask for it. And asking for more information is a buying signal. The rule here is uncluttered, simple, and clear.

JOSETTE: *I was working with a marketing company on their employees' presentation skills. One person got up to do their bit with PowerPoint and went through slide after slide, each with four graphs to a page. She had charts for everything - you name it, she had a figure for it. Everyone, including those from her department, was utterly lost. I asked her to go away and come back with only the bottom-line information. The next day she came back with just two slides: one with a graph and one with a chart. When I asked how she felt about her new version, she stated that it was even clearer to her now.*

So remember, a presentation with PowerPoint . . .

- Is a promotional tool for you, your Company and your product. Use your logo wisely

- Is a visual reinforcement and aid to emphasise your key points

- Is a visual way of sharing complex information. Just remember to keep graphs simple. As we have said, your audience will ask for more information if they are interested

- Is a selling aid

- Is a way of keeping people interested in what you are saying. An audience's eyes wander, and however good-looking you might be, they won't want to stare at you constantly for 20 minutes. This gives them somewhere else to glance, but keeps them focused on the matter in hand

However, it is . . .

- Not a substitute for talking to your audience

- Not a visual script of what you are saying – in other words, full sentences that your audience can read along with as you speak, or an excuse for you to avoid learning your presentation

- Not an art gallery. Remember, relevant pictures only!

- Not an excuse to put up every chart you can think of to prove your point

- Not the sum total of your knowledge. You need to know more than you are showing on the screen

JOSETTE: *There is a fantastic American comedian called Don McMillan who includes in his act a skit called 'Life After Death by PowerPoint'. You can find an extract on the web. Why do I draw your attention to this? Well, he may be hysterically funny, but his observations are also spot on. Watch, laugh, and learn!*

EXERCISE

Look at these examples of PowerPoint slides. Which do you consider to be good and which do you consider to be not so good?

Why?

What should your slide look like?

Consider areas such as:

- ❑ The number of bullet points
- ❑ Background colour
- ❑ Font type and colour

Other thoughts . . .

- ❑ Would a picture enhance your message?
- ❑ Could you embed a video?
- ❑ What would be the benefits?

- Some people like to put their information up in a long sentence, which means their audience is now concentrating on what they are reading, not what you are saying

- You could talk about pink elephants after a while because they would be so busy reading this that they wouldn't really know what you'd said . . .

- These people also like to read from the slide - which means turning their back on the audience . . . which doesn't really matter because the audience no-longer cares about what they are saying or doing anyway

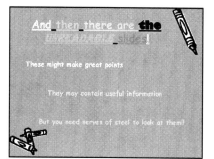

And then there are the UNREADABLE slides!

These might make great points

They may contain useful information

But you need nerves of steel to look at them!

The Rules

1. Choose your font carefully
2. **USE A CLEAN AND SIMPLE LAYOUT**
3. Don't write in clashing colours
4. **Don't use a clashing background colour**
5. Keep chart and diagrams simple
6. Spel cheque
7. Then cheque IT buy eye

Preparing for a demonstration

If your product is highly demonstrable, you must show it off in the best possible light. Whilst a good demonstration can finalise a sale, a poor demonstration will certainly stop a sale completely. Preparation and anticipation are important here.

Consider *why* you are demonstrating your product. The answer is that, by demonstrating a product, it will often sell itself better than you can. Think: "See it to believe it". People won't necessary take you at your word. What you say is subjective. Seeing something for themselves will always be more convincing.

Consider *how* you are going to demonstrate your product. In what order will you show its features and benefits? Consider why you are doing them in that order. Is there a logical progression to this order? More importantly, are you making the greatest impact?

If your product uses accessories, what might the customer ask about them? Consider how you could demonstrate these.

Then think about what might go wrong. What are your product's idiosyncrasies? We hate to undermine your wonderful merchandise but, for example, if your product is electrical, will it overheat if it's going to be left on for 20+ minutes? Be ready to turn it off in between talking and demonstrating. What about your environment? Do you have extension leads in case there is no socket close enough? Could you run it on batteries if there is no power at all? Think everything through and prepare for as much as you possibly can. It won't rain if you carry that umbrella.

You don't have to demonstrate everything; the trick here is to be relevant. Demonstrate the parts of your product that will be of most interest to your prospect and their company.

Finally, practise, practise, practise!

EXERCISE

Use Worksheet 5: Demonstrating

List the key features and benefits that you wish to show off in your demonstration.

Against each of these, note the considerations (what you need to do to show these off). Then write down any potential pitfalls involved.

Gathering evidence for your services and skills

Clearly, there are products that cannot be demonstrated, and this applies particularly to services. If you are selling insurance, pensions, IT support, visionary services - in fact, anything that can't be physically shown - there are other ways of demonstrating the benefits.

Here are some useful questions to ask yourself so that you can promote and prove your service:

- Do I have testimonials from satisfied clients?

- What results can I quote?

- What past jobs can I refer to?

- What case studies do I have?

And the more independent the proof, the greater its impact:

- Can I provide performance figures?

- Are there magazine articles that might serve me? For example: an independent review of my service or product.

- Are there any survey results that back up my sales pitch?

If you do have any of the above, are they in an accessible format? Can you produce a handout or report (a powerful way of getting the point across)?

EXERCISE

Use Worksheet 6: Proving Your Service or Skill

Consider what evidential support you can provide for your service or skill-set. Use any of the appropriate examples given, and then add some of your own. Against each one, list what you have available, or could source in the future.

N.B. Not every example heading will apply to everyone. There is also space for you to add your own proof.

Preparing for Q&A sessions

The fear of actually doing a presentation is one thing, but often those who are confident enough about standing up and presenting still fear being asked questions. It is important to remember that questions are actually a buying signal. Once again, the solution is to be well prepared. Anticipate the questions you are going to get, then prepare the answers associated with them. When questions are answered well, they can increase the chances of a sale dramatically.

So, what types of questions could you get? Let's look at some of the more commonly asked questions. These are applicable to nearly all sales situations.

- What is the price/how much do you charge?

- When can it be delivered/when can you start?

- Can you deliver/start sooner?

- Do you have a returns policy?

- What happens if it goes wrong?

- What guarantees can you provide?

- How long will it last?

- How long has it been on the market/how long have you been providing this service?

- How good is your record in this area?

- Have you worked with similar companies?

- Have you been trained to do this?

- How long have you been providing this service?

All of these give you the chance to reiterate the benefits of your product or service.

As we have said, you can always try to pre-empt questions by covering them in the presentation itself, but there is always a chance that someone will miss the point you have made, or that they will deliberately want you to restate the answer.

EXERCISE

Use Worksheet 7: Preparing for Q&As

We have re-listed the questions above. Write your answer to each of them. There is also space to add and answer your own questions, which you know are common to your industry.

Prepare for the questions you don't want

You should be able to answer all of the above; otherwise your clients may wonder why you are selling your product, or why you are in business.

But what about the questions you *don't* want? Questions such as:

- Can you do a deal?

- I read a report/internet review/article that said your product was terrible, what do you have to say?

- The last product you sold us had all sorts of problems, why should we use you again?

- How do your competitors compare with you?

- Why should we trust what you are saying?

Worse still, what about really contentious issues? For example, a competitor has a faster delivery time, your service doesn't cover all geographical areas, and the equipment overheats if left on all night. It is not unusual for a salesperson to have something that they hope potential buyers won't pick up on, but sticking your head in the sand and hoping that the audience don't know about it or won't bring it up is quite simply asking for trouble.

Naturally, you will avoid stating any negatives in your presentation. But don't avoid thinking about them. Sod's law says that at least one person in your audience will ask you about just those negatives. So, do you have answers to the questions you *don't* want?

Prepare good strong answers, ideally positives, to deflect them. For example, a competitor may have a faster delivery time, but the benefits of your service are that you will set up the equipment, saving the customer time, effort and manpower (or womanpower). Do you have any evidence to support your response - facts, figures or research?

There is a whole section on Q&A sessions, but preparing for the worst is one of the key elements of making the best out of a bad situation, so preparing answers is a critical part of a successful sales presentation. And, as with everything else, make sure your answers are succinct.

EXERCISE

Use Worksheet 8: Preparing for questions you don't *want*

Write down the worst question a prospect could ask you during your presentation. Don't stick your head in the sand – be honest with yourself.

Then write the best answer you would be able to give them. Remember the example quoted above. Finally, do you have any evidence to support your response?

Now consider what else they could ask you and repeat the exercise.

Practising to get the best results

There is no doubt in our minds that practice makes perfect. But how should you practise? We have three suggestions for you, but there are two key points we should make first:

1. You should *always* practise your presentation out loud. Why? Because you are linking the mental with the physical. Have you ever wanted to say something and it has not come out right? By using your voice, moving your lips and tongue, you are making sure that your thought process and physical production are in sync. Once you have said something out loud, it is easier to say a second time. You will never find an actor who has not done vocal, tongue and lip exercises before they go on stage.

2. Most presentations are made whilst standing up. Therefore, always do your practice standing up - unless you absolutely know that this would not happen in reality.

So, our three alternatives:

1. Practise in front of a mirror. This is useful for seeing what you are doing with your facial expressions and your body language.

   PETER: *This is my preferred method. This is partly because, as a busy person, I don't have time to ask others to listen to me, and partly because personal appearance and mannerisms are important aspects of my rehearsal process. I look at myself and ask: "Would I buy from this person?"*

2. Visualise your audience and practise presenting to them, gestures et al. Picturing your audience allows you to build your confidence, practise your mannerisms, project your voice and, by imagining faces (or at least silhouettes), practise looking at them eye to eye (this is your eye-line). Plus, it won't be such a shock when you suddenly find yourself in a room full of people.

   JOSETTE: *This is my preferred method. It allows me to imagine either specific people, or faceless people (depending on whether I know any of my audience). I see the approximate number of people in a room, which I hope will resemble the one I'm going to be in terms of size and layout. It's not an exact science, but by the time I do the presentation, my environment and my audience actually feel quite familiar.*

3. Practise in front of a friend or colleague. This allows you to have a real audience (great if you find visualisation more difficult), regulate your voice, and receive feedback both visually as you deliver your presentation, and verbally, afterwards. You can also ask them to practise a Q&A session with you.

CHAPTER 3

Choosing Words that Influence

Much has been bandied about when it comes to verbal versus non-verbal communication. A classic example is that 7% of communication comes from the actual words you use, whilst 38% comes from other vocal cues such as intonation, pace, pitch, volume, and so on. A significant 55% is considered to be non-verbal communication (body language, for example).

The original research behind these statistics was carried out by American psychologist Dr. Albert Mehrabian. He was looking at emotional responses as part of a much more in-depth study of non-verbal communication in social interaction. His initial reference was to *facial* expression, not body language per se.

So where does the reference to body language come from? Well, this seems to be based on a later statement in which Mehrabian generalises that any implicit behaviour can affect the overall impact of someone's message. That can be anything from their posture and gestures to eye contact and facial expression which, along with other vocal cues, can actually outweigh the words we use.

What you do physically can undermine what you say. However, if you look at it from the other side, it can also support what you say, which is why we cover body language and physicality throughout this book.

This also makes the words you *do* use even more important. As a salesperson, you should not only choose your words carefully, you should make sure you select them for the greatest impact.

The effects of the language we use

It was Kipling who said that words influence people in ways that can sometimes be quite spectacular. Even the subtlest differences in the language you choose can have a really strong impact.

Consider these two phrases: "people find" versus "you will find". The first is generic and shows no connection with your audience. The second encompasses your audience. It's a subtle difference, but one which either includes or excludes your potential clients. As an example, you may use the former when you are about to give evidence: "People find that our product really saves them time. Here is an example . . .." This is okay, but now look at: "*You* will find that our product can really save *you* time. Here is an example . . ." Now you are talking to your audience about what your product does for *them*.

Another consideration is what we call the "hope factor". Of course, you are hoping that your audience will like your product, like you, and like your presentation. But expressing that out loud will give the impression that you lack confidence - and that, in turn, will reflect on your pitch, and your product. Consider the following phrases:

1. I *hope* you like our product.

2. I *think* you'll like our product.

3. You *will* like our product!

4. I *believe* you will like our product.

5. I *know* you'll like this product.

What message does each of these convey? Say them out loud.

We think you'll agree that the first two are very wishy-washy phrases. They show a lack of positivity, and will do nothing to convince your audience or promote your product or service.

The third option may work in certain countries, but it is positive to the point of aggression. British companies tend to find such directness an instant turn-off. We Brits do not enjoy an evangelistic approach.

Now consider the fourth option. This is far more appropriate -you are showing a belief in your product. This is very strong, and very influential.

However, strongest of all is the phrase "I *know* you'll like this product". Of course, you must make sure you follow this with key benefits, but knowing something is a very powerful message for you audience to hear. What more can a client ask?

It is not for us to put words into your mouth, but do think very carefully about the words you choose and the subtleties attached to them. There is a reason that officials in the public eye have advisors and speechwriters who sit and consider every word they will say. Your audience is *your* public. Make sure you are always appropriate with your language, and consider the nuances of the words you use.

For example, do you ever use negative phrasing to make a point?

"We may not be the biggest supplier, but we do provide one of the best services in the area."

It's something everyone has done – pointed out a negative and justified it. Of course, if you know that your customer already has a concern, then addressing that worry up front is an excellent strategy. However, you do not want to put ideas into their head that weren't actually there in the first place. Why not just say:

"We provide one of the best services in the area"?

It is the power of suggestion. In the same way, if you tell your audience that you "don't lower standards"; you have suggested low standards to them. The positive suggestion would be a phrase such as: "We have the highest standards". The lesson here? Use appropriate language which shows that you have confidence in your product.

JOSETTE: *A classic example of this is a salesman who felt it necessary to tell a potential customer that his machine did not come in black yet. What was the colour that stuck in the customer's mind? You guessed it - they wanted to know when they could get the machine in black!*

If that weren't enough, talking in negatives generally reflects back on the person speaking. People who speak negatively are perceived as negative people. So talk positively about yourself and your product.

Formal versus informal language

How often have you listened to a presentation and found it rather starchy? It may have been interesting, it may have made its point, and you may well have enjoyed it, but the language the presenter had been using didn't quite seem natural.

This type of reaction is usually brought about by another linguistic pitfall - the use of formal language, often used in written reports, rather than natural speech.

We will talk about delivery later in the book, but when you write your presentation, it is important to remember that you will be speaking the words, and so putting down your thoughts in the same way as you would an essay or a report does not really work. The trick here is to use *natural* language.

A presentation is, in essence, a conversation. You are simply the one speaking at this point, and your audience is listening. Therefore, your language should reflect this. Phrases such as: "You will observe . . ." are too formal and much more suited to a formal document. In real life, you would say to someone: "You can see . . ."

Report-speak: "Notwithstanding". Natural speech: "Despite".

Report-speak: "I concede". Natural speech: "I admit" or "It's true that".

By using natural language, you are making it easier for your audience to listen to you, to buy into what you are saying, and you are building a much better rapport with them.

How to build a rapport with words

This brings us on to another point. Try this: next time you walk into a room, make a mental note of the very first thing that you notice. Was it the layout or the colour scheme, for example? Was it how noisy or quiet the room was? Perhaps it was how warm or cold it was, or maybe the smell? Or were you just too busy thinking about your meeting to notice any of the above?

Different people notice different things, and Neuro Linguistic Programming (NLP), a system developed in America by professors John Grinder and Richard Bandler, defines six different represent-ational systems which reflect this: visual, auditory, kinaesthetic, olfactory, gustatory, and auditory digital.

The person who notices the layout or colour scheme may have a preference for visual information. The person who notices whether a room is noisy or quiet is most probably auditory – they tend to take in more information through listening. People who reflect on the temperature of a room, or the speed at which people entered are more physically aware, and they would be classed as kinaesthetic. The person who notices the smell? They are using their olfactory sense. The person who was too busy thinking to notice anything would be considered auditory digital.

Some people view NLP as more of a pseudo science, but much of it does reflect accepted principles of psychology. And, of course, most people utilise several senses simultaneously. However if, as we noted earlier, 80% of people really are visual learners, it is most likely that your audience will have a preference for visually expressed information.

So, what does this have to do with effective language? Well, NLP would argue that the language we use tends to reflect our representational system. For example, someone who is visual may ask to "see" or "view" more of your product, and might respond with "That looks good". Someone who favours the auditory system might ask to "hear" or "discuss" more about it. They might respond with "That sounds good". A kinaesthetic person, who is physically aware, expresses this by asking to "explore" things further or talk about the "effects". They would use phrases such as "You've certainly grabbed my attention". Whilst someone who is more thought-based (audio digital) will want to make sense of what you are saying and wish to "understand" more or "consider" the benefits. Their turn of phrase would be something such as "You've anticipated our requirements very well". The other two systems are less prominent, but you may hear someone say that they "smell a rat" – which means they are displaying olfactory tendencies or, if they say they have a "thirst for knowledge" - you guessed it, they are using gustatory (taste) terminology.

From a presentation perspective, using language that resonates with your audience is key to building a rapport and establishing buy-in. Remember earlier we spoke about making an impact during your introduction? One of the examples was to ask your audience to "imagine" their brochures, whilst the other was to "think" about their sales.

If you work in perfumes or food, clearly you will be talking about smell and taste. At the other end of the spectrum, if you are working with science labs, your language will be based around processes and logic.

Another aspect to consider is the language associated with the benefits of your product or service, and to sell those with appropriate language, too. A dress may initially appear to be something visual, but the 'feel' of the material may be a strong selling point - or the sound (taffeta rustles), or even the smell, if that dress is made of leather. The key here is to vary your language to cater for the various preferences in your audience.

JOSETTE: *I worked as a guest presenter on a shopping channel. For several years, I sold a well-known juicer. Each time I appeared, I would juice every fruit and vegetable I could think of. But my audience could only see what I was doing. So, I made a point of always sipping my concoctions and telling everyone how great they tasted. And then I would refer to the delightful aromas – the wonderfully fresh apple smell; the beautiful scent of oranges. The point is that I was expanding my audience's experience of my product.*

One tip here is that if you have had the opportunity to talk to members of your audience previously, note their language – and therefore their preferred representational system. Then try to incorporate it into your presentation. But remember, no one will use a single system 100% of the time.

> ## EXERCISE
>
> We have looked at what you noticed going into a room. Now listen to how you speak (or record yourself chatting to someone), and consider the words you favour. Look at your written work as well – that can also be very telling. Do you have a preferred representational system? Which is it? You may find that you have to adapt your natural language when you present.

The 3 Cs of Communication

Finally, have you considered exactly *how* you communicate? You may have heard of 'The 3 Cs of Communication' or 'The 3 Cs of

Effective Communication'. The interesting thing is that there seems to be no definitive agreement on what these three Cs actually are. Here are a few variations we found that you can mull over:

- Clear . . . Concise . . . Consistent

- Correct . . . Concise . . . Complete

- Clarity . . . Consistency . . . Confidence

- Crisp & Clear . . . Customer-centric . . . Consistent

- Clear . . . Concise . . . Convincing

Our choice?

Well, we are split. From a presentation perspective, clear, concise and consistent are obviously paramount. However, from a sales perspective, no one will buy from you if they are not convinced of the benefits.

The power of rhetorical questions

Although presenting, by its nature, is about delivering information, there is a time when you will actually interact with your audience. This is during the Q&A, when the discourse becomes two-way. However, you can also engage your audience verbally, without actually having a conversation. We are talking about the rhetorical question.

You will often hear good presenters throw out a question to their audience. Actually, they may not want either an answer or a discussion at this point. Instead, their aim is to simply make their audience sit up and take notice.

Throwing out a rhetorical question can make your audience more alert, build a rapport, and maybe even give some of them an adrenalin rush (usually because they momentarily jump at the thought that they may have to speak). It is, in fact, a way of verbally engaging your audience without them saying a word.

As we mentioned, this is Peter's favourite way to start a sales presentation. In a sales environment, a rhetorical question should be about your audience's needs or requirements. For example, if you are pitching something with the benefit of no paper wastage, you could ask: "How much money do you lose through paper wastage?" Give them a second for impact, and then give them the answer: "Companies such as yours can spend millions unnecessarily, but with this product/service . . ."

This works in the same way if you have a service or skill to sell. A web designer might ask something along the lines of: "What do you feel potential clients think of your current website?" Again, give them a second and then provide the answer: "Companies such as yours rely on your website to drive customers to make enquiries. I looked at your website and it seems to be missing some key elements. We are able to provide . . ."

What you are doing is planting a need in their mind, and providing a resolution with your product, service or skill.

As effective as this technique is, though, it does come with warnings. Firstly, you should always make sure of your prospect's requirements. Just because you have a machine with a specific benefit, does not mean it is a major deciding factor for every potential client. Do your research ahead of time, and make sure that any questions you throw out really are important to them – and that you have the correct answer with an appropriate benefit.

Secondly, when using this technique - and we will presume that you *are* only using a rhetorical question - if they do give you an answer, acknowledge any response and move straight on to your killer benefit. If you don't, asking a question, even a rhetorical one, can result in a discussion which you might not want to have at this point. It can also use up valuable time, may put your presentation out of sync, and will possibly dilute your impact. That is why we recommend using closed questions, so that you are more likely to receive a simple "Yes" or a "No", if audience members do answer you.

It is also best to limit how often you use a rhetorical question. Too many times, and your audience will not only get wise to what you are doing, they will get fed up with it. We suggest keeping it to two or three, at most.

JOSETTE: *You may have attended external seminars with several speakers providing insight into their area of expertise – for example, marketing your brand. Each speaker will provide you with some key learning, which will both whet your appetite and prove their ability to you. They will then go on to sell you something – another workshop, for example. In this scenario, a speaker will actively encourage you to answer them by continually asking you 'yes/no' questions. Many will actually get you to raise your hand as you agree with them. All of this is a way of compounding your buy-in.*

It is only fair to advise you that, in our experience, this technique is not in any way beneficial in a corporate sales environment or bidding process. In fact, it can be quite detrimental.

EXERCISE

Use Worksheet 9: Rhetorical Questions

Consider what rhetorical question you can ask during your presentation . . . and then answer this with a benefit.

Repeat the exercise and choose the best ones for your presentation.

CHAPTER 4

Delivering on the Day

So, you have done all of your preparation, designed your best possible presentation, refined your content to within an inch of its life, polished your language, and the demonstration/proving part is organised. Oh yes, and you have practised, practised and practised again. Now all you have to do is stand up in front of your audience and deliver your pitch.

But the truth is that your presentation starts well before you open your mouth. Social scientists believe that people will form a lasting impression about someone almost instantly. There has been a tremendous amount of research in this area (you can find some reading in our bibliography), and results vary - but not that much. By 'instant', these scientists are quoting anything from the first nine seconds up to around 30 seconds. Whatever the reality, it is an extremely short period of time.

Worse still, research by psychologist Aleksandr Kogan and his colleagues at the University of California suggests that, based on non-verbal behaviour, it takes just 20 seconds for someone to decide if a stranger is trustworthy or not - a pretty important perception for someone going into a sales situation! Furthermore, researchers Janine Willis and Alexander Todorov of Princeton University did a whole series of experiments which suggested that looking at a stranger's face for just 10 seconds was enough to form an opinion.

This sort of research is ongoing and varied, but the overriding message for any salesperson is that you are being judged from the moment a prospect sets eye on you. And it is imperative to remember that this may not be during the presentation itself.

There are three basic scenarios to consider. In the first, you are greeted in reception by your host – who is potentially a member of your audience. In the second, you are brought into a room to meet your prospects and you will then give your presentation. And in the third, you will be setting up and they will come into the room to see you.

The point here is to treat the whole process of meeting, greeting, and setting up as part of the presentation. You don't know the position of the person who has come to help you, or what influence they have within the company. Of course, be polite and courteous to everyone, but also be aware of any throwaway or negative remarks you might make. If you've been stuck on a train or in traffic, don't complain or moan. By all means apologise if you are late, but keep a positive and charming disposition. We've seen salespeople tutting away as they lay out their demonstration, complain that their product doesn't seem to be working properly, and even make inappropriate comments such as, "Oh well, no one will notice."

Remember, however your meeting starts, you are already being assessed.

Choosing the right thing to wear

There are no two ways about it - you will be judged on what you wear. Clothes send a subtle message about you, and by default, about the company you represent and the product or service you provide. Always look businesslike, neat and tidy, clean and well groomed. That does not mean be boring, but do consider the impact you are making when you choose your clothes.

Certainly, some people like to be a little flamboyant or quirky, whilst others deliberately dress to distract. But think carefully before doing either of these when presenting to a potential client. Wearing that jovial animal print tie with an orange shirt is not going to make anyone take you seriously. If you are female, it is no crime to wear a skirt above the knee or a v-neck top, but how far above the knee and how low a neckline should be considered with care. You are there to enhance your product or service, not take the limelight away from it.

In the same way, a shabby suit or scuffed shoes screams shabby product or service – and certainly a lack of attention to detail. Would you trust someone who doesn't maintain their own appearance to maintain their product to a particularly high spec, or to provide a well maintained service?

There are plenty of experts out there who can help you with your wardrobe – and that includes shop assistants, but our advice is, if you're not sure whether you should wear something – you probably shouldn't!

And don't be fooled. It doesn't matter what your prospective client is wearing – they can dress in jeans and a furry hat – you are the one who needs to make the right impression.

As a guideline, we would suggest that you try to dress one step above your potential client. So if they are in jeans, you are smart-casual. But if in doubt, it is always better to be too smart rather than shabby.

PETER: *I used to have a banking client who was always dressed very smartly. In this case, I made a point of wearing my very best suit, and I always wore a professional looking tie and polished my shoes until I could see my face in them!*

JOSETTE: *As a woman, I always like to admire other women's taste, and dressing to a similar level or one step above does tend to work well. When I train women in presentation skills, I will always point out two pitfalls in particular. The first is perfume. Speaking to a woman wearing heavy perfume is very off-putting, so keep it subtle. The second area is jewellery. There is nothing more distracting than jangly bracelets, or trying to* *focus on someone wearing a large piece of jewellery that is reflecting light at you.*

From another perspective, you should also consider whether your product or service, or for that matter your surroundings, call for specialist clothing. If you are working with food, then wear the appropriate garments and hair covering to fulfill health concerns. If you are working with something that requires safety equipment to be worn, such as goggles, gloves, and helmets, make sure you are wearing these for your demonstration. Remember that you are setting the safety standards for your client. This is about being professional at every turn.

And finally, if you are going into a restricted area, always check what you can and can't wear - for example, high heels or sandals on factory floors.

How to present with confidence

From the moment you walk into a room, greet a prospective client, or stand up to give your presentation, it is important to come over as confident and in control. People buy from confident people because confidence (although *not* cockiness) is nearly always taken as a sign of ability.

If you are someone who struggles with nerves, this is where you can lose out. Get into a nervous state of mind and that's exactly how you will come across. You may not even be aware of what you are doing, but the most common giveaways include shuffling your feet, transferring weight from one foot to the other, clasping your hands tightly together, rubbing your palms together (a subconscious way of getting rid of sweat), self-soothing (stroking your own arm is an example of this), slouching shoulders, drooping your head slightly, dropping eye contact, licking your lips or pursing them tightly together, and swallowing a lot - and that's just meeting your potential clients. Once you start your presentation, you can add a shaky voice, speaking too high, speaking too fast, hesitating, nervous laughter, avoiding looking at your audience, twisting watches and bracelets (or just a bare wrist if you have taken them off), and for men, the infernal jangling of keys or coins in your pocket.

Yet it is not necessary. There really are so many ways of dealing with, and dissipating, nerves. Different methods work for different people, so let us look at a few of the more basic techniques.

Presumptions

A lot of nervousness or lack of confidence stems from focusing on your audience and worrying about their perceptions of you. Asking yourself: "Will I get the sale?" or worse, telling yourself that you will "Never get the sale" is counter-productive. You don't have to pretend that you can do no wrong, but realise that if you do your best, you have the best possible chance of making a sale.

In addition, there is a reason that you are there. Companies do not have time to waste, and you are not there because they are doing you a favour. You are there because they want to hear what you have to say and offer. Prepare well, and concentrate on your messages and your objectives.

And never, ever, assume you know what your audience is thinking. Someone frowning may suddenly have remembered they have to make a phone call later.

Deep breathing

We have all been told to "breathe deeply" at one time or another, but what does that mean, why do we do it and, most importantly, does it work?

Someone who is nervous will tend to take shorter, sharper breaths, which means they are breathing more shallowly, high in their chest, usually raising their shoulders as they do it. Tell them to "breathe deeply", and they will merely take in more air high in their chest.

So, what do we really mean by "breathe deeply"? The error is in the description, not the idea. What you need is to breathe deeply *down* into your lungs, inhaling and exhaling slowly. This is often referred to as breathing into, or from, your diaphragm, in the same way as actors and singers do. (There is more on this in the Vocal Delivery section). This lower breathing can help to slow down the rate of your breathing, which in turn has a calming affect.

EXERCISE

Lie on your back. Relax. Breathe normally. Now place your hand on your stomach and continue to breathe in a normal and relaxed state. Can you feel your diaphragm falling and rising? That is normal breathing, and that is where and how you want to be breathing when you are standing up presenting. If you take a deep breath, it should be down into this area. Then exhale very slowly. Repeat this a few times, and you will feel calmer.

The fascinating thing here is that bad, shallow breathing can actually make you feel nervous, even when you're not. Try it for yourself. Inhale air, but only into the top part of your chest so that you can see your chest rising up and down. How do you feel? Probably a bit heady, as well!

What this shows us is that not only can your mind affect your body, but that your body can influence your mind. Nervous breathing equals a nervous you. Relaxed breathing equals a relaxed you. And this is true of your body language.

Body language

Your body language reflects your emotional state, and vice-versa. Stand with your shoulders slouched over, look at the floor, fidget . . . you will feel unconfident. Stand up straight, with your shoulders back, chin level, stomach pulled in, and you will feel more confident. So use your body language to reduce your nerves.

In the same way, pacing up and down aimlessly, consistently moving your stance, and in particular, rocking backwards and forwards whilst you are talking to your audience will send a message of insecurity to your brain. Placing your feet firmly on the floor with your weight evenly distributed will make you less fidgety and, again, help you to feel more confident. Opera singers stand with their feet shoulder-width apart with one foot very slightly forward, because it feels very secure to stand like this. Exactly where you place your feet is an individual choice, so do experiment to see which position stops you from rocking or shifting about.

Similarly, gripping onto things such as a lectern can also cause you to feel unnecessary anxiety, by sending a message of insecurity to your brain. Relaxing your grip relieves tension in your arms and throughout the rest of your body and, in turn, relaxes your mind, making you less stressed.

A secondary result of this is that, apart from *feeling* calmer and more confident on the inside, from an audience's perspective you will also *appear* more confident. And if you look confident, your audience will have more confidence in you - and what you have to say which, in turn, increases your power to influence their decision making process.

Smile

We are not talking about an inane grin here, but research has shown that by mimicking a positive/happy facial expression, your brain believes that you are in a positive frame of mind. Reverse this and frown, and your brain interprets sadness and negativity.

EXERCISE

Try it for yourself. Force yourself to smile for five minutes as you go about your business. How do you feel?

Now do the reverse - frown, pull down the sides of your mouth and look miserable for five minutes. How do you feel now?

There is always an excuse to smile. When you first take up your position to present, why not smile and nod at your audience – not only will you feel better, but you will have started rapport building at the same time.

Of course, you don't have to smile continuously, but there will always be a point during your presentation when you can at least lift the corners of your mouth.

In addition, research by Marc Mehu of the Swiss National Center of Competence in Research Affective Sciences has shown that smiling could be an important factor in forming and maintaining co-operative relationships.

Ways to engage and influence your audience

So, what exactly is 'engaging your audience'? Quite simply, this is about building rapport - the sort of rapport that you would have when talking to somebody any day of the week. It comes from the words you use, how you say them, the way you stand, your eye contact, your gestures and your body language.

And by building rapport, you are then able to influence people. There are three main categories:

- Verbal influence

- Physical interaction

- Vocal delivery

Verbal influence

The words you use have a lot of power, which is why we dedicated the whole of the previous chapter to choosing your words and analysing the language you will use.

Physical interaction

We have spoken about how confident body language can not only help you, but influence your audience's confidence in you. So let us now look at how your physical behaviour can influence your audience.

Movement

When we talk about movement, it can be broken down into two parts: firstly, moving around your presentation area, and secondly, gesturing. We will cover gesturing in a moment.

For the nervous, standing firm and looking confident is important, but movement during a presentation is *not* a sin. It just has to be for a purpose and, used properly in the right environment, it is a great tool for engaging with your audience.

In a corporate environment such as a defence bid, you will as often as not find yourself in quite a small presentation area, speaking to just a handful of people. In this scenario, movement is not actually a necessity and wandering around can make you look restless and nervous. Besides which, if you get too close to your prospective customers, it can make them feel uncomfortable. To this end, in smaller presentation areas, we suggest that you stand in one place, to keep your appearance natural.

If you are presenting in a larger space such as an exhibition stage, moving around can actually be beneficial if used in the right way. Using your space well can allow you to engage more closely with your audience. This in turn enables you to 'work the room'.

So, what do we mean by 'work the room'? Well, watch any good comedian. If they are in an intimate venue, they will stay fairly centred. Put them onto a large stage, and they will ensure that they move from one side to the other to interact with as many of their audience as possible. What they are doing is moving with intent, and one way of doing this is to make eye contact with people on the other side of the audience and move over to address them and those around them.

Which brings us on to:

Eye contact

One of the great mistakes people make during presentations is to believe that they are in a theatrical production. In the theatrical world, you do not look your audience in the eye. Thespians are trained to talk out to the back of the auditorium or into the 'gods' whilst their (hopefully) adoring audience watches them in awe. The audience is looking in, even drawn in, but an actor does not interact with them, and most importantly, will not build direct rapport. Presenting is not the same as theatre in this context, and you are actually relying on direct rapport to make your sale.

Of course, making eye contact can be nerve racking, especially if you look at someone and don't get what you consider to be a positive reaction. Let's face it - how many times have you stood up and spoken, only to find that some people simply won't look at you, or are sitting with their arms crossed looking dour, whilst others seem so engaged, nod and (shock, horror) may even smile? Who do you find yourself talking to? It is natural to go for the people who seem to be receiving you well. However, you may end up excluding some important people in your audience if you only focus on the happy-looking ones. On top of this, you will eventually unnerve those with friendly faces if you consistently focus on them.

JOSETTE: *It is very tempting to read crossed arms as closed body language, and vacant looks as negative thoughts. Some people just* *like to sit like that, whilst others may be processing what you're saying and do not feel the need to show any emotion. Do not judge your audience. How many times have you finished a presentation, and then found to your surprise that someone who had looked disinterested throughout the whole thing has come up to you and been very positive?*

The trick is to look at everyone at some point. And remember, you will never win people over if you don't look at or talk to them.

A good rule of thumb is, when you are in front of a larger audience, make eye contact with an individual for about four or five seconds, or the length of a phrase, and then move on. A plus here is that when you look at one person some way away, those around them will often think you're looking at them, as well. Work in a systematic, but not obvious pattern. By all means work left to right, for example, but it is often more effective to work in a zigzag. That way your interaction does not look contrived.

In a much smaller audience, you can take that up to around six seconds. This allows you to work around the whole audience in a balanced way and is usually quite comfortable from both sides.

Finally, if you are pausing for thought, look up or ahead, not down in order to keep your audience engaged, and your projected confidence steady. Looking down can draw your head down, and you will not only lose eye contact with your audience, it can also send a nervous negative message to your brain.

Gestures

Another way of building an audience's confidence in you, and therefore your influence over them, is through your gestures. Wild gesticulating can be very off-putting, but a lack of gestures can have the same effect. We have seen so many presenters who have been 'trained' and now think that they must keep their arms down and their hands still. But that is not normal for anyone, and presenting is about having a conversation with your audience – and a certain amount of gesturing is natural.

So the answer is to be aware of your gestures, and use them to emphasise and complement what you say.

As examples, open hands with palms up or forwards shows honesty and openness.

Making the okay sign to make a point is very clever - it is subconsciously sending a positive (okay) message. Great influencers use this all the time.

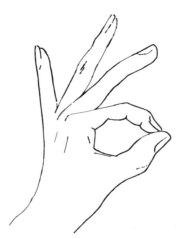

Pointing is seldom acceptable, so politicians, and good presenters, will use the 'thumb on top' gesture with a closed hand to drive a point home.

Showing the back of your hand with your thumb up and a more open hand is also a strong gesture and sends a message of positivity (thumbs up).

In fact, watch any well trained politician and you will see an artist at work. Look and learn.

But do remember, gestures are a cultural thing, and there are many normal British gestures which are unknown or unacceptable to other nationalities. Please, please do your research if you are presenting abroad or to a multicultural audience.

Vocal delivery

One of our pet hates is the confusion between public speaking and presenting. Certainly, public speaking skills can be a useful part of improving someone's delivery, and we certainly cover these below.

However, some aspects of public speaking are detrimental to giving a successful presentation – particularly in a sales environment. Public speakers often slow down their rate of speech, become theatrical in their manner, and tend to over-exaggerate the way they talk. They orate, and this can make their presentation sound more like a speech . . . not a good idea, unless you are a member of the British Royal Family!

Presentations are about engaging your audience, building rapport, building trust and, in this instance, making a sale. What an effective presenter does is speak relatively normally. American author and trainer Rob Sherman wrote in the U.S. magazine *Business Credit* that you cannot connect with your audience without authenticity, and that means speaking in a natural, more conversational tone.

The 5 Ps of Vocal Impact

Good vocal delivery is essential, and we use the 5 Ps of Presenting:

- Pace
- Pitch
- Pause
- Power
- Points

Pace

Many people, even without attending public speaking seminars, will find themselves talking far more slowly when they stand up to do a presentation. If you are one of those, ask yourself what happens when you watch a presentation where someone is speaking very slowly and deliberately. Our guess is that your mind wanders.

That is not to say that enunciation and articulation aren't important - they are paramount, but speaking too slowly leaves your audience with time on their hands, attention diminishes, and they become easily distracted. Research by psychologist Neal Miller and his colleagues found that people who speak more quickly are actually more persuasive. Slower rates of speech were seen as an indication of submissiveness, and those speakers were deemed less persuasive, more passive, and weaker.

On the other hand, speaking too fast can also be problematic. Not only can you lose your audience because they can't keep up, they will not be able to process the valuable information you are imparting.

In 1922, BBC Radio Director of Programmes Arthur Burrows conducted an experiment to find out what rate of speech was most comfortable for listeners, and on 14 November that year, he read out each bulletin twice – once quickly and once slowly. He then asked listeners to say which version they preferred. The rate they chose dictates, to this day, the speed at which most newsreaders across Britain present their bulletins. It is 180 words per minute.

180 words per minute works out at around three words per second. (Obviously, this is a guide, as some words have a lot more syllables than others.)

EXERCISE

Use Worksheets 10: Two-Minute Presentation

If you are wondering about your own speech, use this Worksheet to write out a presentation of 360 words – one word per box. Each section is made up of 90 words which should equal approximately 30 seconds each. Next, practise saying it out loud, whilst timing yourself. At a rate of 180 words per minute, the presentation should take two minutes.

If you are a lot slower, or a lot faster, adjust your rate of speech and try again. Practise until you find a speed that is closer to that rate.

Pause

It is important to recognise that when we talk about words per minute, that does not mean you cannot pause. Pausing is a very effective way of making an impact. It also helps you to gather your thoughts, avoids "umms" and "errrs", and actually gives your audience time to digest what you are saying.

The best place to take a pause is at the end of a sentence. Compare:

"As you can see, this product has superb dongles. It is, errr, most effective . . ."

Versus:

"As you can see, this product has superb dongles." PAUSE – gather your thoughts. *"It is most effective . . ."*

If the sentence is really long though, pause at the end of natural phrases.

"As you can see," PAUSE *"This product has superb dongles."* PAUSE *"It is most effective . . ."*

Pitch

Intonation is very succinctly described by renowned phonetician Prof. John Wells as the "melody of speech". And within that, we are looking at how the pitch of the voice rises and falls. By varying your pitch, you are actually enhancing your vocal delivery, and that is key to holding your audience's attention.

Let us be brutal here - talking in a constant monotone will soon leave your audience disengaged and bored. Remember, the word monotonous comes from monotone, and a voice which drones on will soon lose your audience. In fact, research by David Addington, a Professor of Speech and Drama shows that monotonous voices are judged as less credible and less persuasive.

What you are looking for is an intonation that moves with a nice variation - not exaggerated and theatrical, just varied, and above all, enthusiastic. This will not only keep your audience interested, it will make you sound more interesting.

JOSETTE: *Banking executive, Toast Master and author Herbert Prochnow wrote a wonderful book in 1951 called* The Successful Speaker's Handbook. *He summed up many of these points under the heading of 'Manifesting your Enthusiasm'. For me, that says it all.*

Pitch is how high or how low your voice sounds – and it has been found that someone with a higher pitched voice was judged by those listening to be more submissive, and appear nervous. In fact, in the U.S. it was discovered that people would be more likely to vote for electoral candidates with a deeper voice, regardless of their sex. No one is saying you should become a bass baritone, but what you are looking for here is gravitas.

JOSETTE: *For women, a high-pitched voice can be somewhat disadvantageous when trying to exert influence. To gain respect, many high profile females have lowered their pitch. A prime example of this is former British Prime Minister Baroness*

Thatcher, who did not start out with the low tone of voice we always associated her with.

Power

Try holding your breath and talking . . . yes, it's impossible! Some sounds are produced purely by using escaping air and making shapes with your lips, mouth and tongue – these are known as 'voiceless' sounds. Try hissing. The 'ssss' sound is voiceless. There are other sounds that are made in the same way, but which also incorporate the vocal folds. These vocal folds vibrate as the air passes over them. That sound is termed as 'voiced'. Try buzzing like a bee (yes, really!). The 'zzzz' is voiced.

If you can't hear the difference, gently place your fingers across the front of your throat. Can you feel the difference? Nothing happens with the 'sss', but you should feel vibration when you make the 'zzz' sound. (By the way, all vowels are voiced. Try saying 'ee' on its own, without any vocalisation. You're just expelling air, but there is no actual sound.)

So, why are we telling you this? Well, using your breath not only helps you to produce sounds, it also affects how loudly or softly you speak. And volume (the power of your voice) is very important in making an impact. Louder speech is judged to be more persuasive and more influential. Somewhat unsurprisingly then, quieter voices are quite simply less persuasive.

This does not mean that you have to shout. We are talking about projecting your voice. Speaking 'out' if you like. When you produce a sound, it is carried by the air you exhale.

Earlier, we said we would explain more about breathing into the diaphragm. All professional actors and singers are taught to 'breathe' into their diaphragm and lower rib cage (known as floating ribs or false ribs), expanding the local muscles as they do so. They are then told to exhale by contracting these muscles slowly and releasing the air in a controlled manner. Clearly, no one inhales air into their diaphragm or ribs, but by describing breathing in this way, the process is more easily visualised. Using this method allows for better breath control, better airflow, and as a consequence, greater volume.

Try these exercises. The first is about controlling your breathing, and the second should show you how your breathing helps your volume.

EXERCISE

Place the palms of your hands just above your waist, either side of your lower ribs. Breathe down into the area, and as you do so, try and push out your hands. Then very slowly exhale, releasing the air from there first, and feeling your hands moving back in.

What you're doing is trying to slowly squeeze the air out in a controlled fashion. Pulling in your stomach gradually can help you do this.

EXERCISE

Pretend you want to get the attention of a taxi or perhaps attract a friend's attention across the road. Just call out "Taxi!" or "Hey!". I guarantee that you managed quite a lot of volume without really 'shouting'. Now try again and try and be aware of what your diaphragmatic muscles and lower ribs are doing as you do this. That is the sort of control you would use to project your voice.

We have seen that deeper breathing is helpful when dealing with nerves. But now we know that it is also very important for voice production and clarity of voice. In the same way that taking in shallow breaths (high in your chest) can cause you to feel nervous, inhibiting air flow also affects your ability to produce any real volume.

There is just one further piece of advice here: consistency. Keep your voice constant. Many people fall into the trap of speaking out beautifully, but then they trail off into nothingness at the end of a sentence. Finish each phrase or sentence just as firmly as you started it. This makes communication clearer, conveys confidence and, in turn, makes you a lot more effective.

Points

To make an impact, you should always highlight your most salient points. One way of doing this is to emphasise the most important words.

If it is not immediately obvious to you which words are important, you are looking for those that are informative, sell your product, and will influence the sale.

As an example: "*This computer has an unrivalled 425 inputs. Our nearest competitor's has just 207.*"

If we analyse the emphasised words in this example, you are clearly indicating *your* computer, rather than any other, and you have stressed that the inputs are unrivalled, but the most important figure, the astounding 425, is ignored.

Let's look at another version: "*This computer has an unrivalled 425 inputs. Our nearest competitor's has just 207.*"

By emphasising both numbers in this example, you are leaving them with the 207 strongly in their mind – particularly as it is the final figure. The importance of the 425, even though you emphasised it, is lost.

66

Now look at: "*This computer has an <u>unrivalled</u> <u>425</u> <u>inputs</u>. Our nearest competitor's has just 207.*"

You have indicated your enthusiasm for the computer, highlighted that it is unrivalled, and left them with your incredible number emphasized. But then you have carried on talking, rather burying the point.

Now compare the impact if you swap the phrases: "*Our nearest competitor has just 207 <u>inputs</u>. <u>Our</u> computer has an <u>unrivalled</u> <u>425</u>.*"

You have highlighted immediately what you are talking about by emphasising the first "inputs", so this is 'old news' and does not have to be re-emphasised. You have then finished by emphasising "our computer" and ending on an impactful "unrivalled 425".

So, the key is to ask yourself, what do I want the audience to remember? Then make sure you emphasise those points and arrange your sentence to best effect as well.

EXERCISE

Try saying a sentence and emphasise different words. Record yourself if you can and see which has the most impact.

Now to take that a step further, consider what would happen if you put the sentence another way around. Remember, it is always worth playing around with sentence structure, as well as the emphasis.

In summary, by considering all of these aspects, you will make your presentation lively and stimulating, and create a more interesting experience for your audience. But more importantly, you will keep your audience engaged, come over with conviction and passion, and subtly influence and persuade them. All clear winners in the sales stakes.

Using written prompts in a presentation

Probably one of the biggest questions is whether to use notes, write a script or simply learn a presentation by rote. Each of these is valid in its own way, but actually we do have a preferred method, and that is to work from bullet points. Let's discuss each of the options, because what suits one person may not suit another.

Using some form of aide-mémoire during a presentation is in no way a bad thing. Certainly, it is vital to know your facts inside out, but a presentation is not a memory test, and it is better to have a prompt than to leave out a key piece of information in the heat of the moment.

Of course, there are those who prefer to learn a script verbatim. But a word of caution - if you are not a trained actor, repeating learned words can sound recited, dry and unconvincing. What's more, we have witnessed presenters dry up and stumble because they have suddenly realised that they have missed something out. So this method is not really recommended. If you still believe this is the only way forward for you, here are a few tips:

- Watch your speed. When someone knows something by heart, they often speak too quickly

- Ensure you vary your intonation

- If you make a mistake, carry on. The audience has no idea what you meant to say!

At the other end of the scale are those who like to *read* a script verbatim. Again, we don't consider this the best method. You are losing eye contact with your audience for long periods of time, which goes hand in hand with losing their attention. Plus, reading can sound boring and monotone. (It also hints that you might not know about the subject you are presenting.) If you really have to read whole sentences, then there are three key points to remember:

1. Make sure that you have used the sort of words you would *speak*, not the sort of words you would write in a report. We have a whole section on formal vs. informal language, and never is it as true as for those who are presenting from notes.

   If writing in a 'speaking' style doesn't come naturally to you, simply reverse the process. Rather than writing what you want to say, say it first and record yourself. Then write that down.

2. Don't keep your head down as though you are reading at school. There are some techniques used by actors which can help: Try to scan around five words ahead, so that you can keep looking up. You can keep your place by resting the fingers of one hand on the page, and using them to fix your place when you look up.

3. Remember to vary your intonation. If you find you have become monotone, put some marks on your paper to remind you to vary your pitch and emphasis. One method is to underline the key words.

In between are those people who like to use informal notes. These can be very useful, and we are not totally discounting them. However, from what we have seen, a lot of these notes are not as helpful as they could be. Scribbled ideas can be hard to access when you are under pressure, and jotting down your long sentences can leave you searching for the salient points.

Having suggested what we don't recommend, what do we suggest? The answer is: bullet points. By writing down bullet points to prompt you, you will be able to speak in a much more natural way. Glancing at this type of aide-mémoire from time to time allows you to fully engage with your audience and demonstrate freely. It also means that you can be flexible with your content, including or excluding information as you see fit. For example, if you arrive to find that your audience has more knowledge than you were led to believe, or that they have less knowledge, you can adapt accordingly. In the first instance, you might be able to provide more advanced or more technical information. In the second, you may wish to add in more basic background information. This is not so easy to do if you are reading from a script, searching for the salient sentence or reciting a speech.

One question we are regularly asked is how to create relevant bullet points. There are several methods, but we have two that we recommend. The first is to write out your presentation in your usual way, highlight your key points, and then cut these down to make bullet points. Clearly, this is very time-consuming, but some people feel safer working from this amount of detail.

The second, and speedier, method is to make a diagrammatic chart and then translate this into bullet points. There are several types of diagrams which you could use. Peter prefers mind-mapping, whilst Josette uses a spider diagram.

EXERCISE

Use Worksheet 11a & 11b: Developing salient bullet points

Look Worksheet 11a. Draw a diagrammatic chart (of your choice) for your presentation.

Finally, use Worksheet 11b to turn your chart into bullet points.

Speaking 'Off the Cuff'

A step on from speaking with bullet points is speaking 'off the cuff' i.e. with no notes at all. This allows for total audience engagement. But do not be deceived - speaking off the cuff is not just about knowing your product, and it is certainly not about making it up as you go along. Remember at the beginning of the book we talked about the benefits of standardising presentations?

Speaking off the cuff comes from experience, in-depth knowledge, and a *lot* of practice. If you are new to sales presentations, your organisation, or simply standing up and speaking in front of an audience, this is not something we would recommend.

Those who are good at speaking without notes are already competent presenters, have learned to be concise and can self-edit. They are able to progress what they are saying logically and in a structured manner - and this is no mean feat. Speaking off the cuff and still giving every part of your presentation a beginning, a middle and an end, takes great awareness.

Yes, these presenters make mistakes and forget things, but they are simply polished enough not to show it. On the other hand, those who are bad at it waffle, have no effective structure, and can fail to make some of their most important points, losing their audience - and their sale.

At the end of the day, your aim is to communicate your message effectively and either progress or make that sale. Getting praise for talking without notes is of no benefit to you or your business.

For those of you who believe you are ready and would like to work without any notes, we would suggest working from bullet points initially and then moving on. This should give you a good structure and help you commit the format of your presentation to memory.

Making the most of visual aids

If you are using PowerPoint or any other visuals, there are a few things to keep in mind. For a start, one of the most common practices is to turn around and look at your slides, even when you have a computer screen in front of you. Doing this means you lose eye contact, and therefore connection with your audience. To engage with your audience, you need to be speaking directly to them, so unless you are checking a problem with your slide, it really is best to keep facing forward. The only exception to this is if you wish to focus your audience's attention on the screen, for example to look at a chart or an embedded video.

In the same vein, do be aware that if you turn away from your audience for any reason, you should stop talking. They cannot hear you, unless you are miked up. Even then, if you are wearing a lapel mic, turning your head away from the side on which it is fastened, means your voice will not be picked up clearly. If you need to turn your back, for example to walk over to something, do it with aplomb and the audience will wait with interest to see/hear what comes next. Remember, a pause can be positive. One useful accessory is a 'clicker'(a device which allows you to move slides on without touching your computer keyboard). This means you are free to move away from your computer without interrupting your flow.

One plea . . . please, do not read your slides verbatim. You should know more than your slide and be able to expand on your bullet points. In turn, this will enable you to customise your comments to your audience.

The same rules apply to any video footage you may choose to include. Do not be tempted to talk over or comment during the video, and if you wish to reiterate anything from it, only highlight the key points.

Don't be afraid to pause your PowerPoint to direct attention to you or your product. Press B for a black screen, W for a white screen. Say what you have to say, and then go back to your slides.

And finally, finish with the audience's focus on you or your product, not the PowerPoint. You are there to make a sale, and that cannot be done with your audience staring at a slide. Case in point is during your Q&A session, when you need their attention focused on your answers (which we would hope are reiterating key benefits!). You have a couple of options here. You can design a slide that does not detract from you, such as one saying "Q&A"

or "Questions Please". You can show your logo, or you can blank the screen.

All of the above points we have raised for PowerPoint are also relevant to using flipcharts.

In a sales presentation, there are three main ways of incorporating a flipchart:

1. The pre-prepared flipchart. This is where you will have written your key points in advance, in a similar way to a PowerPoint presentation. However, don't prepare too many. This is *not* PowerPoint, and the constant flipping of paper can become annoying.

    You may even wish to use a flipchart as a backup to your presentation, to reinforce a point.

    PETER: *I will often put something such as the presentation agenda on a flipchart. This means that when I am running through my presentation on PowerPoint, my audiences don't forget what I will be covering. The benefit here is that you curtail questions around points you will be getting to later.*

    JOSETTE: *Some people will even put their name, position and company up on a flipchart, so that you don't forget who is talking. It's little trick that motivational speaker Anthony Robbins has used in the past.*

2. The 'write as you go' flipchart. This is very useful for explaining points or diagrams in small chunks to prevent the audience from having to decipher something complicated in one go. This works by adding information systematically and explaining each part as you go.

    But remember what we said about turning your back and talking. This is a sales presentation, and you need to engage your audience. We would also add that to look professional, writing as you go along can be perceived as being unprepared.

3. Ghosting. Some presenters do try to use a flipchart as an aide-mémoire, and we have observed people who have lightly pencilled words onto their sheets because this cannot be seen by an audience. Ghosting one word where you want to write something, or outlining a diagram to ensure accuracy, is a clever technique.

    However, don't end up using pencil prompts as a replacement for your presentation notes. This will leave you constantly turning your back to your audience. So, think carefully about how you use this technique.

CHAPTER 5

Proving yours is the best!

'Proving' or the process of providing evidential support, whether you are asked to do so by a prospect or not, is an essential part of the sales cycle. Most good sales training companies will cover this subject area in a course, but often will not specifically cover demonstrations. However, we believe that demonstrating and proving your product or service is of major significance and can make or break your chance of a sale.

Demonstrating your product or service

If your product or service is demonstrable, then show it off! There is no better 'proof' that your product works the way you say it should than a first-class demonstration. (Equally, a poor demonstration can easily put back the decision process, or even wreck your sale completely.)

How to demonstrate

The techniques involved in delivering a sales *demonstration* are often very different from those required for a sales presentation. When we talked through doing a PowerPoint presentation, we discussed that slides should be designed to support, not distract from you the presenter. However, in the case of the demonstration, it is the product that should get the attention.

In addition, a presentation will normally direct an audience to ask questions at the end. On the other hand, a demonstration will often incite questions, and it is usually best to provide practical answers where possible. We will discuss that later.

On the plus side, like any other presentation, demonstrating is all about planning and practice. In both cases, it is important that you know your product extremely well so as to show it off in the best possible way.

If you have a product present, it is important to plan ahead. Ask yourself what will show off your product in the best possible light. Is it the speed? Is there something unique about this product, its design or size? You know your product well - what are its strongest features? Are there any Unique Selling Points (USPs) which put it above its rivals – ones that you can demonstrate?

Ask yourself simply, what are the major benefits of your product, and how are you going to show them to the prospect?

PETER: *A trick used by car manufacturers is to demonstrate their top of the range model. One of the benefits here is that it avoids trivial questions such as: "Does it come with a satnav?", which can interrupt your flow and stop you from concentrating on the real sales benefits. In addition, clients are actually more likely to buy the model that is being demonstrated.*

If it is difficult to show off your product, there may be ways of showing it by using video footage, a dummy or even a metaphor. There is the example of a salesman who was selling packaging equipment designed to protect large, fragile objects being shipped overseas. To demonstrate it, he used small versions of the materials to wrap a delicate porcelain bust before placing it in a small box. He then asked his prospect if he felt comfortable about shipping his possessions in this way. The prospect could see the example was directly relevant and placed the order.

Finally, consider the negatives (and be honest!). Is your product quite complex to operate? Does it have any major flaws, such as overheating? If it is difficult to operate, practise until you are slick. If it has a flaw such as overheating, time your demonstration to avoid this happening.

What we are saying here is: plan your demonstration well, so that it is as easy and trouble-free as possible. Then practise, practise, practise to make your demonstration the best that it can possibly be.

But what if you want to demonstrate your product without having it in situ? Well, people often use photos, but one of the best ways to do this is visually through the medium of video. Think of the safety demonstration on a plane.

PETER: *One of the best examples I have seen of this was a video animation that was presented to potential investors in the construction of the new Hong Kong airport. The video demonstrated how passenger flow would be achieved with the new building design. The production was clever, engaging, and showed in detail the workings of the airport before a single brick was laid.*

In some cases, a video can completely replace a demonstration. However, you would need pretty impactful video content to achieve this. If you do go the video route, it is important to apply the same rules as any other part of your presentation, including shaping it into a logical and progressive structure, highlighting benefits, and avoiding superfluous information and waffle.

The demonstration area

One major aspect of your sales demonstration is its location. For example, if you are doing it at your own premises, consider the immediate environment. If the area surrounding your product is noisy, messy or distracting, then you need to attend to that.

If your product can be demonstrated at your prospect's site, take it there. Seeing a product in situ can often persuade someone to purchase it, particularly if they are highly visual. Perhaps you'll make a sale, and be able to leave your product there when you leave.

But again, consider the environment. Arrive at the site early, so that you can compensate for any potential issues. Check the position of power points, for example. Does your lead reach? Do you need an extension cable? Are there any health and safety issues? Be prepared for every eventuality, and don't be afraid to rearrange the surrounding area to suit you. Ask for furniture or clutter to be moved or removed to give you space. Ask for chairs for those attending; it is to your benefit to keep your audience comfortable and focused on the product. If chairs are already laid out, don't be afraid to move them to give the best view of your product.

One other point is lighting. If you are using PowerPoint or video, can your audience read the screen, or is it being blurred out by either sunlight or electric lights? Check before you start.

And if you are using audio or video, consider the sound quality. Check whether you will be able to plug into a sound system in the room. And do sound checks before you start. If you know you will use audio or video on a regular basis in your presentation, it might even be worth investing in some external speakers.

Remember, this may be your only chance to demonstrate, so make sure that your demonstration area isn't the area that sabotages you.

Delivering a demonstration

The star of a sales demonstration is your product and not you, so remember to treat it like one. Demonstrated properly, your product is not only going to provide your customer with proof of its benefits, it should also pre-empt many questions. Indeed, if a prospect asks a question, you can literally turn to your product and demonstrate the answer. Repeatedly guiding the audience to the product allows the product itself to do the convincing.

PETER: *Some companies encourage their staff to be positive towards their equipment all the time. A certain well-known copier* *manufacturer would encourage its sales staff to treat their copiers 'lovingly,' even to the point of putting their arms affectionately on them whilst demonstrating.*

You may not wish to hug your equipment, but positivity is catching and sends a subtle message to your prospects about your product.

Another useful technique is to create some excitement. Give your product a build-up and even cover it under a sheet, revealing it in all its glory when the right moment comes.

Next, should you let a prospect touch the product in a demonstration? The general school of thought is to demonstrate the product yourself first, as you know its strengths best. But as anyone selling a car knows, getting a prospective customer personally involved by sitting them inside a car, so that they can bond with it through touch and feel, can do more than all the talking in the world.

PETER: *There is a lovely combination of NLP and rhetorical questions used by car salespeople. They will seat a prospect in a new car and say: "It smells good, doesn't it?"*

So, whether you are demonstrating a motor car or a new computer, there is a lot to be said for letting the prospect try something for himself. However, although this can be a useful sales technique, as can lending out a product, be aware that it may cause problems too.

Anticipating problems

It goes without saying that the more complex your product, the higher the likelihood that something might go wrong. If the product is not working well, stay calm. You may kick it when you're back at the office, but don't show any negative reactions to your audience. In fact, if you can rectify the problem quickly, or distract them by moving to another part of the demonstration, they may be unaware that you are even having a problem.

We mentioned before that practice is so important, and by practising you will, hopefully, discover any scenarios that might cause a problem. If nothing shows up, don't rest on your laurels – do some checking. A little research will tell you if there are any weaknesses in your product. And don't forget - if your prospect is shopping around or doing their research, they may already know of any intrinsic faults.

The other aspect of this is that if you know there is a weakness in the product, should you avoid it during a demonstration? Should you be honest, or should you have a plan in place to circumvent this?

Naturally, if it is a serious problem which addresses exactly the prospect's main requirements, then there seems little point in a demonstration at all. However, where a minor feature of the product is not working properly, it is best to be honest - providing you know, and can confirm, that this point will be addressed by your company. Again, remember that your potential customer may already be aware of any weaknesses or intrinsic problems.

We cannot act as your moral compass, but there is a big difference between selling a prospect something substandard and not to their requirements, and overcoming minor negatives with other suitable benefits.

What to do if it goes wrong

There may be no substitute for planning and practising, but even the best demonstrations can go wrong. There can be silly accidents like a spillage, or a host of influences outside your own control that affect the demonstration itself.

Again, having alternative plans can be advantageous. The types of accident or influences are too numerous to mention, but here are some ideas, just in case:

- Have a second product to hand and ready to demonstrate

- Have another venue in mind to demonstrate the product, possibly that of a satisfied customer

- Highlight your maintenance and training offerings on the product

- Have documentary proof of your product's reliability

JOSETTE: *As a sales demonstrator on a well-known shopping channel for several years, I learned very quickly that machines like to blow up at the most inappropriate times. On my first-ever show I used one demo machine which overheated in the first eight minutes. I could even see smoke coming out of it!*

I couldn't continue what I was doing, so I moved to the items I had produced from the product and showed them off whilst continuing my pitch. No one seemed to notice, and I sold out. After that, I had three spares lined up. Of course, I made sure they didn't look like spares. I laid them out in different states: one assembled, one open, and one disassembled. Any problems with one, and I simply moved to another machine and carried on as if it were part of my original plan.

Showing off your services and skills

The best type of proving is to provide a sales demonstration. When a prospect asks: "Can it do that?", physical proof will answer that question best. However, not everything can be demonstrated, and this is true of many services and skill-sets.

That does not mean that you cannot prove the value of what you are offering. Proving is about providing evidential support to show the worth of a product, service or skill.

So, what happens if you a selling a service or skill that cannot be demonstrated? Or if something goes wrong with your demonstration, and you cannot show off your product? Well, there are a number of recognised materials that can be used to prove what you are offering. Here are some examples:

- Case studies of your product, service or skill

- Testimonials/customer quotes complimenting your product, service, skill or company

- Supporting video footage

- Names and information of satisfied customers (possibly to contact)

- Independent reports/reviews

- Magazine/newspaper articles about your product

- Performance statistics

- User guides

- Company history/statistics

- Brochures

All of which, you should have available for your prospects to view. Of those listed, testimonials and customer quotes tend to remain one of the most powerful proofs.

JOSETTE: *There is an annual international survey produced by independent PR Agency, Edelman. Called Edelman's Trust Barometer, the survey measures how people view the credibility of different businesses and institutions. One of the areas they look at is who we trust, and includes everyone from an academic or 'expert' to a CEO or industry analyst. The results are very useful if you are deliberating over whose testimonial will add the greatest weight to your product or service.*

But do not overload your audience with information. If you provide too much, they will simply shut down, and this will negate the effectiveness of what you are showing them. You may find that much of your proof is not actually required during your presentation. It is one thing to anticipate common questions and include them in the body, but it can also be very useful to hold back some of the detail and then use it to support you during the Q&A session. Experience will tell you what is most appropriate for each customer but, as a rule of thumb, try to tailor what you provide to reflect your customer's industry and needs.

CHAPTER 6

Using Q&As to your Benefit

The fear of actually doing a presentation is one thing, but often even those who feel confident in front of an audience still dread being asked questions.

Whether it is within a presentation or as a bid defence, the solution - and we won't stop repeating this - is to be well prepared, anticipate the questions you might get, and have the answers associated with them ready. Crucially though, it is important to realise that being asked a question is, in fact, a buying signal.

If no one actually asks you any questions, you really do need to ask yourself whether you have covered everything they needed to know in your presentation, or whether your audience simply wasn't interested.

We have spoken about asking your audience rhetorical questions, but some presenters will ask questions that are specifically designed to open up a discussion. The idea here is to provide an opportunity for you to highlight or elaborate on a particular feature or benefit of your product or service. You can do this by identifying a problem or need that your client has, and then showing them how you can address this. Or, you might wish to discuss something which you know is unique to them. This then helps them to appreciate that you understand their company and their situation.

PETER: *Both of these examples are quite similar. The difference is that in the first, a salesperson is quite specific and might ask: "After your fire last summer, how long did it take you to retrieve all of your vital information?" The sales person will then highlight the benefits of his or her service. The second scenario is more general, and the question would change slightly to something such as: "Can you tell me what would happen to your data if you had a fire next week?" He or she would then talk about what they can offer the client, and again highlight the benefits of their product or service.*

The only danger here is that your audience can then hijack your discussion and take you completely off track. It takes a strong and confident presenter to keep such a discussion on topic and under control, and then be able to drop back into their presentation. Our advice is: in a sales environment, questions are best left to the end of the presentation - unless you are really sure you can stay in control.

Turning questions to your advantage

It is fascinating to note that, in the sales process, answering questions is actually very similar to the techniques used in handling objections. Both show audience engagement, both allow you the opportunity to reiterate your benefits, and both allow you to progress your sale.

As with handling an objection, firstly make sure that you understand the question and repeat it if necessary. This is not only for your own clarification; in an audience environment, it could be that others have not heard the question at all. (It can also give you thinking time.)

If you know your audience, then you can answer the question as you prepared it or to the best of your knowledge. As you do so, tie in and reiterate the benefits of your product or service.

Check that you have answered the question and, where possible, confirm that the decision makers in the room appear to have understood as well. Good question answering can often lead more quickly to a sale.

If you do not know the audience, you are quite entitled to ask how that person is involved or affected by the question that they raise. This can provide you with important insight into why they have asked the question, any underlying motive, and the sort of answer which would best satisfy them.

We have already discussed the preparation of the obvious questions that are applicable to nearly all sales situations, but always be ready to answer less obvious questions, such as:

- Have you got any references?

- Can we speak to any of your clients?

- Will you negotiate on the price?

With regard to references, the answer should be "yes". Make sure that you have organised these ahead of time.

Involving clients can be difficult. If you do have a client who is willing to do this on your behalf, get their permission up front. Even the friendliest of clients will not want to be pestered, particularly if they are not expecting a call.

When discussing price, know where your negotiating points and your margins are. Only then can you even begin to answer.

And remember, all of these questions give you the chance to reiterate the benefits of your product.

Dealing with objections and difficult questions

We asked you to ensure that you prepare for the questions you don't really want, because burying your head in the sand does not mean that someone won't ask you. But what if the questions you get are just plain awkward, such as:

- I read a review which said your product did not perform/ compared unfavourably/was not up to scratch - is this true?

- The last product you sold us didn't work. What will be different this time?

- How do your competitors compare with you?

- Why should we trust what you are saying?

While these may not be the exact wording, these four questions are typical themes that need to be answered. As a guideline:

- *An unfavourable review*

  Whether it's online, in print or on TV, the power of the internet is such that it can turn one bad review (whatever its source) into a disaster. Try and read as many reviews as you can pertaining to your product, company or yourself for that matter. You need to be able to understand how bad the situation really is to help you prepare your answer. Then make sure you can provide other reviews or proving statements to counter any negative criticism.

- *It didn't work last time*

  Provide research and case studies to show how your product has been improved, and how well this new one will perform.

- *Competitors*

  Never be nasty about your competitors, highlight your USPs, and concentrate on being positive about yourself, rather than negative about your competitors. (Remember what we said about negative comments reflecting back on you.)

- *Trust*

  Relate company history, company performance, and provide quotes from satisfied customers.

But what if you really are stuck? What if answering the question directly and honestly will actually harm your sale? First and foremost, do not lie or make anything up. There are ways and means of moving on.

Always acknowledge the question. Not doing so or ignoring it will only anger the person asking the question, which means they will a) repeat the question, only louder, b) stop listening to you whilst they smoulder and focus more and more on their own negative thoughts and/or c) bring it up outside of your presentation to someone else, causing a snowball effect. Nip it in the bud.

Ways of acknowledging a question vary from repeating the question (always a good idea, in case you have misunderstood it), to thanking the questioner for bringing the point up.

Next, find something you can work with within the question and focus on that, not the negative aspect. Then finish with a positive and a link back to any relevant benefits. For example, if they say that they have read research that completely undermines your product, pick up on the word "research", and use it to link to some positive research, perhaps from another source. For instance: "Thank you for that. We are delighted to report that recent research by X shows that our product has actually performed exceedingly well. This research was backed up by . . .", and then give a reference/third party testimonial, and go back to a benefit if you can.

The key here is to remain unfazed, stay pleasant and welcome their question. The audience will react to the way that you react. If you become defensive, nervous or annoyed, this will tell your audience that the questioner has touched on a nerve or something negative. By staying positive, you will help alleviate any concerns and keep your audience on side. This is also a good time to move on to other benefits and other aspects of proving.

Do note that this is the one time you should *not* go back and ask if you have answered their question. If they are still unhappy, they will soon let you know. If they have gone along with your answer and moved on, asking them to analyse what you have said is simply rehashing any negativity, and encouraging further analysis. Again, this will not just stir up the person asking the question; it will affect your whole audience.

And now for a bit about body language. We have said that 55% of your communication is through body language/facial expression. With this in mind, be very aware that your physical reaction can belie your words. A negative question will often produce defensive body language in the presenter. This can include: averting eyes/ losing eye contact, folding the arms, fidgeting, finger-twitching (pressing fingers together for example), foot-twitching, shuffling, a sudden straightening of the spine, an intake of breath, pursing the lips, or a 'dead' smile (showing the teeth in a smile whilst the eyes stay cold, which in the animal world would be seen as a snarl).

Try to keep your face and body calm, yet confident. Keep your head held high and maintain eye contact with your questioner and your audience.

Think of a poker player - see if you can identify your 'tells' (or ask someone else to) and neutralise them. Staying calm is not easy under pressure, but keeping your body relaxed is achievable with practice. And let's face it, if there is something about your product or company which could come into question, you should already know about it, so why the surprise?

Handling vacuous interruptions or questions

There are, of course, those in the audience who just want to show off their own knowledge, or like to be the centre of attention whatever the circumstances. They might interrupt or they may bring up things that are totally irrelevant or inappropriate. This may come in the form of a statement that doesn't actually require an answer, a question or, to be brutal, a waffled monologue.

Your choices are either a) to take whatever they say as an 'in' to get out one of your key messages or b) to just thank them for their insight, and carry on with what you were saying.

If they bring something up of which you are unaware or to which you have no answer, again, you can thank them politely and say that you will look into it and come back to them – preferably giving a time frame.

Remember, whatever happens you are aiming to make a sale, so politeness is of the utmost importance. If anyone brings something up which is correct but irrelevant, you can take the opportunity to publicly acknowledge their expertise, but then move on. Don't be afraid to politely halt them if they are taking up valuable time and not enhancing your sales opportunity.

JOSETTE: *We have experienced this more than once, often to our amusement. One case in point was during a seminar, when literally two slides in, an audience member interjected to tell us that "tone of voice" was very important in a presentation. Because this was my area, I thanked him and complimented him on his observation, explained that we would indeed be covering this, and then went back to what we were talking about. When it came to the section on vocal delivery, I acknowledged the gentleman. The point here is that it is not about one-upmanship or control, but keeping the presentation on track, and your audience on side.*

CHAPTER 7

Making that Sale!

We have established that a sales presentation is an important step in the sales process. However, all too often, someone will do a brilliant presentation and then sit down, perhaps even to applause, without advancing towards a sale in any way.

As with any sales process, how you finish your presentation is crucial. Correctly done, it gives you both the opportunity to progress the sale to the next stage, and offers you the chance of a Trial Close – a technique we will explain later.

There are many discussions on this subject. In the 1950s, sales trainer and author Charles Roth suggested that a presenter should spend 25% of their time on handling objections and closing. In other words, to differentiate a *sales* presentation from any other type, you need to spend 25% of it on the 'business end'.

Too often, and particularly where a sales presentation has technical content, too much time is spent on the technicalities, but little or no time is actually spent on selling or moving a sale forward. Sadly, technical presenters can be the worst in this area because, from a technical perspective, getting the facts and jargon out may make a good, and even interesting, technical presentation. But that does not mean a sale.

In fact, high-performing salespeople believe it is possible to close a sale at any time. Indeed, you can start your presentation with an appropriate close. For example: "Good morning, are you here to buy a house today?" (You can simply insert whatever your product is.) This approach has been known to achieve surprising results.

Of course, it is also a question of style and circumstance, but a close is most often attempted at the end of a presentation. You may even wish to do a Trial Close before the Q&A and a second close afterwards. There really is no rule here.

How the end of a sales presentation is actually worded will depend on what the goal of your presentation is, and this must never be forgotten.

How to progress your sale

At the end of your presentation, you may not actually be in a position to close a sale. Your objective may in fact, be to move on to the next stage of the sales cycle. This can include being put onto a shortlist, a follow-up demonstration, a client visit, or a meeting with the decision maker to discuss the terms of the sale. In each of these scenarios, you should ensure that you always finish your presentation on a strong note. Make it something memorable.

For example, if your client has come to you this time, suggest that you go to them next, so that you can investigate their requirements further.

If you have not had the opportunity to demonstrate a product, suggesting a time and place for a demonstration might be a logical next step in your sales process.

In the same way, if you want to progress a sale by meeting with the decision maker after your presentation, you need to ask for that meeting then and there. It is not sufficient to simply stop the presentation and hope you can corner him or her later.

The end of your presentation gives you the perfect opportunity to encourage this to happen - so use it. In other words, whatever you want them to do at the end, ask for it!

The best ways to close a sale there and then

The Close is essentially asking for the order or asking for the sale to be agreed. Sadly, even the most experienced salespeople forget to close - yet this is essentially the essence of what selling is about.

So how realistic is it to close a sale as part of a presentation? The answer, of course, depends on a number of variables: the timing in the sales process, the buying cycle of your prospect, whether your product or service lends itself to being bought without further testing or information, and most importantly, who you have in the audience.

A close is best attempted when you are sure of your audience. This might be based on evidence, such a positive comment during your Q&A session. It may be based on gut instinct -never something to be dismissed! Or it may simply be the stage you are at in the sales cycle. But if you have all the decision makers and influencers present, it is recommended that you finish your presentation with some form of Close.

The way in which you ask for the close is a question of personal style, and there are many styles. Interestingly though, these styles seem to come from just three main sources: those that have been developed through experience, those that use psychology, and those that have been deliberately designed by sales trainers.

For example, the Puppy Dog Close is a technique that was developed through experience. We will explain more about this and the other Closes below.

The Handshake Close is an excellent example of applying lay psychology. This is often used in close contact sales. After their pitch or negotiation, a salesman or saleswoman will grab a hesitant prospect's hand and start shaking it whilst saying something like: "That's a deal then. Let's shake on it." This action seems to trigger compliance almost immediately.

If we were to quote a technique that has been specifically designed, then the Xerox Corporation's Personal Selling Skills course developed back in the 1970s is a prime example. In fact, PSS has been so successful that it has now evolved and developed into a brand of well-proven selling techniques still used today.

PETER: *I have to admit that I am a product of Xerox's Personal Selling Skills. So effective is this approach that it has not only helped me to a successful career, it also inspired me to develop my own products and services, designed to help others succeed.*

We are not here to dictate which method you should use. Instead, we have provided a cross-section of sample Closes. Have a look and select the one closest to your own style. But don't be afraid to adapt, expand, develop, or completely reword them to suit you. Who knows - you may develop a successful technique of your own.

The Assumed Close

An Assumed Close makes the assumption that a sale is assured and simply asks for details on how to finalise the agreement. As an example: "You can see this product/service is ideal for your organisation. Who should I talk to about delivering our product/service?"

The Blank Order Close

The Blank Order Close works by presenting an order form to your prospect and asking them to sign on the dotted line. As an example: "I have completed an order form for the product I have just told you about. All that is required now is a signature for you to start benefiting from this purchase."

This type of Close is particularly useful at the end of an external presentation which has multiple prospects, companies or organisations present. The trick here is to have an order form appropriately designed to capture all the necessary information you require to process a sale. This should be circulated amongst the audience for them to complete and sign then and there. This gives you the advantage of taking orders from several customers at one time.

The Puppy Dog Close

Ever been into a pet shop, picked up a cute little animal and then wanted to keep it? Well, experience has shown that leaving a product with someone to try for a while has the same effect. So, if you do have a product (or service) that a prospect can trial, this may be the Close for you.

However, do formalise the terms of the loan/service and be specific with the length of the trial period, to avoid any misunderstandings.

The Sharp Angle Close

The Sharp Angle Close is a way of turning a requirement which your prospect has identified into a benefit, and then using this new angle to ask for a sale.

In other words, you are listening to and honing in on what your audience is saying. As an example, if your audience has been asking a lot of questions about their competitors, such as what they do or buy, then this gives you an extra selling point to use with them: "You're obviously very interested in how your competitors are doing. I recommend you invest in this product right away if you need to stay ahead of them".

The 'T' Close

The origin of The 'T' Close is unclear. It is attributed to a number of different wartime leaders, from Benjamin Franklin to Winston Churchill who is said to have used it often in order to convince fellow colleagues in the War Cabinet. And it lends itself well to a presentation environment.

Simply draw a large 'T' on a flipchart or slide and list the benefits of purchasing your product or service on one side of the vertical line, and any reasons for not buying it on the other side of the vertical line. You can also add what will happen/the outcome of purchasing/not purchasing your product or service. Naturally, you make sure the 'good' list is very much longer. This has a very positive visual effect on your audience.

As an example: "You can clearly see that the advantages of investing in our product far outweigh what will happen if you do not. Let us install it as soon as possible, so that you can start to reap these obvious benefits."

The Timeline Close

This type of Close is very useful when the major benefit of your product or service is the delivery time. For example: "When would you need to start these training courses?" The answer would then lead into you outlining your process of delivery, such as: "Great. If you sign now, we can start implementing the course within your agreed timescale."

The Trial Close

There are many different types of Close, and we have touched on just a few above. But as we mentioned earlier, you do not necessarily have to close at the *end* of your presentation. You can use a Trial Close at any time – provided that you believe it is appropriate, or it 'feels' right. For example, you could try to use this Close when you are getting buying signals from the audience or, conversely, when you are getting little or no reaction from them (the idea being that you have nothing to lose, so you might as well ask and see what happens).

A Trial Close will often throw up questions, but as we have discussed, a question is a buying signal. Often, the question itself will indicate that a Trial Close is appropriate. For example, the question: "How long does it take to deliver?" could be answered by: "If we delivered it within a week, would you be in a position to place the order now?" Or "What guarantees do you offer on your work?" could be answered by: "If I provide you with a written guarantee, would you be in a position to sign a contract now?"

This also demonstrates that incorporating a question of your own can soften the bluntness of your Trial Close. Another example: "I believe our product could benefit your company greatly. Can you think of any reason why it would not?"

In addition to having your normal close prepared for the end of your presentation, you may wish to prepare and practise a Trial Close, so that you can take advantage of a situation should it arise.

If a sale doesn't take place at the time of your presentation, then we would recommend a follow-up within 72 hours. If your presentation has been good, then a Trial Close can still have an 80% chance of a sale. However, after 72 hours, this percentage goes down very dramatically.

EXERCISE

Use Worksheets 12: Closing

Have a go at all of the different types of Close. Some will be more appropriate to you than others, but do try them all just the same.

Then, focus on the one that is most suited to your product, service or skill. Work on it and practise your close.

CHAPTER 8

Over to You!

Our experience over the years has shown us that using the techniques in this book will help you to present yourself, your products or your services in the best possible light. It will also increase your chances of a sale, both in the short and long term.

In addition, the tactics we have suggested are here to help you build on and strengthen your client relations and bring you repeat business over the years.

Now it is time for you to take all of the information we have passed onto you, go out there, give your sales presentation, and come back with a sale!

We have put together a checklist to reflect the key points from this book. Make use of this before you give a presentation. We have left space for you to add your own personal actions.

It only remains for us to wish you every success in the future. We are delighted to have been a part of your journey, but now it is over to you. Good luck!

Check List

I. *Plan*

☐ Check who has been invited

☐ Invite your audience

☐ Set your goals

☐

☐

☐

2. *Prepare*

☐ Shape your presentation

☐ Prepare written prompts

☐ Prepare visuals

☐ Prepare demonstrations

☐ Decide how to present non–demonstrable products

☐ Prepare for your Q&A

☐ Prepare the questions you don't want

☐ Time your presentation

☐

☐

☐

☐

☐

3. Practise!

- ☐ Choose your words and language
- ☐ Practise your demonstration
- ☐
- ☐
- ☐

4. On the day

- ☐ Consider what you are wearing
- ☐ Go out there with confidence
- ☐ Engage your audience
- ☐ Interact with your audience
- ☐ Be aware of your vocal delivery
- ☐ Use your rhetorical questions
- ☐ Make the most of your visuals
- ☐ Demonstrate/prove your product/service/skill
- ☐ Deal with Q&As mindfully
- ☐ Continually sell the benefits!
- ☐ Close or at least progress the sale
- ☐
- ☐
- ☐
- ☐
- ☐

Worksheets

Worksheet 1a

Analysing your Audience

Enter the name and title of the person fulfilling each role (*e.g. John Smith, Technical Director*), and whether they'll be attending your presentation.

Role	Name and Title	Attending Yes/No
Decision Maker		
Influencer/s	1. 2. 3.	1. 2. 3.
User/s	1. 2. 3.	1. 2. 3.
Advisor/s & Expert/s	1. 2. 3.	1. 2. 3.
Ultimate Authority		

Worksheet 1b

Inviting an Audience

Given the opportunity, who else would you like to invite and why?

Role	Name and Title	Why?

Worksheet 2a

Meeting your Sales Presentation Goals

What are your goals or objectives for giving this sales presentation? (*e.g. Make a sale, progress the sale, promote a product for sale later. Or you may have something different in mind.*)

1. My main goal or objective for this presentation is:

2. Other goals or objectives I can achieve are:

3. To achieve my goals or objectives, I need to:

Worksheet 2b

Resources and Actions

In the table below, record the resources and actions required to achieve these goals or objectives.

Action	Resource	Date Completed

Worksheet 3a

Example: Feature, Advantage, Benefit

Here is an example using a photocopier. This should provide you with some ideas for your own product, service or skill.

Feature	Advantage	Benefit
It produces 50 copies per minute	*It is quicker than its competitors*	*It saves time producing copies so quickly*
A full manual is provided	*It is made easy to learn how to use it*	*Users will save time by being able to make copies from the outset*
It is available in many sizes and colours	*It looks good*	*It solves the problem of fitting into the current office design*
It comes with a full Guarantee - any problems and there is a full replacement service	*It will be replaced immediately*	*There will be no loss of print time*
The quality of the copies is really excellent	*Copies are of good enough quality to send to clients*	*This improves our image with our clients*

Worksheet 3b

Feature, Advantage, Benefit

In the table below, now write in the five main Features of your product, service or skill. Then add the associated advantages and benefits of each. *If you are struggling with recognising a benefit, question what you have written with "So what?"*

Feature	Advantage	Benefit

Worksheet 4

Shaping your Sales Presentation

Your sales presentation must have a beginning (intro), middle (body of content), and end (summary and close). Complete the following to help you shape your sales presentation.

The Beginning
My opening line is:
Write an example of your strong beginning:

The Middle
My key messages are:
What supporting evidence do I have?
How will I present my evidence?

The End

My summary points/benefits to reiterate are:

What would you like the audience to do at the end of your presentation?

Worksheet 5

Demonstrating

In Column 1, list the key features and benefits that you wish to show off during your demonstration.

In Column 2, write down what you need to do to show off each particular feature or benefit.

In Column 3, note any potential pitfalls involved with demonstrating your product.

Features & benefits being demonstrated	Considerations	Pitfalls

Worksheet 6

Proving your Service or Skill

In the table below, provide evidential support for your service or skill. Use any of the appropriate examples given, and then add some of your own. Against each one, list whether you have these available, or could source them in the future.

Source	Available Yes/No	Action Required
Testimonials		
Results		
Past clients		
Case studies		
Performance figures		
Magazine articles		
Survey results		

Worksheet 7

Preparing for Q&As

Below are 12 commonly asked questions. Write your answer to each of them. There is also space below to add and answer your own questions which you know are common to your industry.

1. What is the price/How much do you charge?

2. When can it be delivered/When can you start?

3. Can you deliver/start sooner?

4. Do you do have a returns policy?

5. What happens if it goes wrong?

6. What Guarantees can you provide?

7. How long will it last?

8. How long has it been on the market/How long have you been providing this service?

9. How good is your record in this area?

10. Have you worked with similar companies?

11. Have you been trained to do this?

12. What qualifications or credentials do you have?

13.

14.

15.

Worksheet 8

Preparing for Questions you *Don't* Want

Write down the worst question a prospect could ask you during your presentation. Don't stick your head in the sand – be honest with yourself. Then write the best answer you would be able to give them. Finally, do you have any evidence to support your response?

The worst question they could ask me is:
Prepare a good strong answer to the question:
What evidence can you provide?

Now repeat the exercise!

Another question they could ask me is:
Prepare a good strong answer to the question:
What evidence can you provide?

You can do this as many times as necessary to cover all of the worst questions.

Worksheet 9

Rhetorical Questions

Write down a rhetorical question you could ask during your presentation. Then answer this with a benefit.

Then consider what other rhetorical questions you could use, and repeat the exercise.

Rhetorical Question	Benefit

Choose one of these, or possibly two, for your presentation.

Worksheet 10

2 Minute Presentation

Write out a presentation of 360 words – one word per box. Each section is made up of 90 words (approximately 30 seconds). Then, practise saying the whole thing out loud, whilst timing yourself. At a rate of 180 words per minute, the presentation should take two minutes.

					30 secs

					1 min

					1 min 30 secs

					2 min

If you are a lot slower, or a lot faster, adjust your rate of speech and try again. Practise until you find a speed that is closer to a rate of 180 word per minute.

Worksheet 11a

Developing Salient Bullet Points 1

Draw a diagrammatical chart for your presentation.

Worksheet 11b

Developing Salient Bullet Points 2

Now turn your diagram into bullet points to use during your presentation.

---

* ....

* ....

* ....

* ....

* ....

* ....

* ....

* ....

* ....

* ....

* ....

* ....

* ....

* ....

* ....

* ....

* ....

Worksheet 12

Closing

Have a go at all of the different types of Close. Some will be more appropriate to you than others, but do try them all just the same.

1. The Assumed Close

Make the assumption that your sale is assured. What question would you ask to confirm that your prospect is ready to go ahead?

2. The Blank Order Close

Prepare an order form that is appropriate to your business. Now prepare what you are going to say to get your prospect to sign on the dotted line.

3. The Puppy Dog Close

What tactics can you use to lend someone your product, or allow them to experience your service or skill?

4. The Sharp Angle Close

Consider a past presentation to a customer. What unique situation or fact specifically relevant to them or their requirements did they highlight? Now consider how you could have used this to convince them to purchase your product, service or skill.

5. The 'T' Close

Use the 'T' below and list the reasons 'for' and 'against' buying your product, service or skill. Make sure the 'for' list is significantly longer!

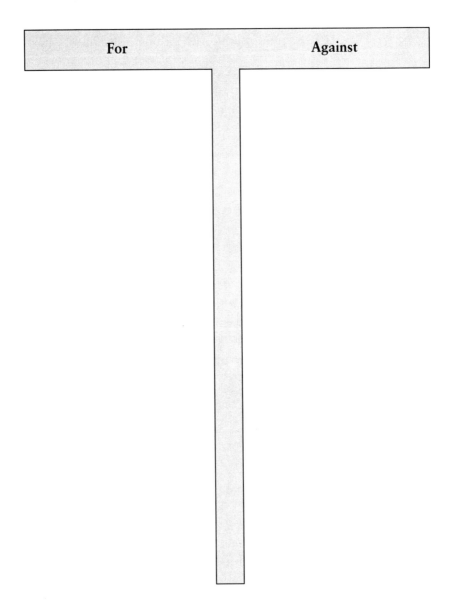

For	Against

Bibliography

Addington, D. W. (1971) "The Effect of Vocal Variation on Ratings of Source Credibility." *Speech Monographs*. 38, 242-247

Apple, W., Steeter L.A., and Kraus, R.M. (1979) in Mehrabian, Albert. (1981) *Silent Messages: Implicit Communication of Emotions and Attitudes*. Wadesworth, California USA.

BBC. (2012) The History of the BBC. http://www.bbc.co.uk/history ofthebbc/innovation/20s_printable.shtml

Buzzotta, V. R., Lefton, R., and Sherberg, M. (1991) *Effective Selling Through Psychology*. Psychological Assoc.

Dukette, Dianne, and Cornish, David (2009) *The Essential 20: Twenty Components of an Excellent Health Care Team*. RoseDog Books.

Edelman, R. (2012) "Edelman Trust Barometer". *Edelman Editions* http://edelmaneditions.com/2012/01/trust-barometer-2012

Hayes, Gareth, Dr. (2005) *Communication and Presentation Skills*. ICR Publishing

Jobler, David, and Lancaster, Geoff (2006) *Selling and Sales Management*. Prentice Hall

Kay, Frances, and Kite, Neilson (2009) *Understanding NLP*. Kogan Page

Klofstad, Casey, Anderson, Rindy, and Peters, Susan (2012) Proceeding of the Royal Society B. Biological Sciences 297, 2698-2704. Duke University N. Caroline

Kogan, Aleksandr, Saslow, Laura R., Impett, Emily A., Oveis, Christopher, Keltner, Dacher, and Rodrigues Saturn, Sarina (2011) "Thin-slicing Study of the Oxytocin Receptor (OXTR)" Gene and the Evaluation and Expression of the Prosocial Disposition Social Sciences - Psychological and Cognitive Sciences - Biological Sciences – Genetics. http://www.pnas.org

Mehrabian, Albert (1981) *Silent Messages: Implicit Communication of Emotions and Attitudes*. Wadesworth Publishing Company, California USA.

Mehrabian, Albert (1972) *Nonverbal Communication*. Chicago, Illinois: Aldine-Atherton. 1972 (a) Chapter 6

Mehrabian, Albert, and Ferris S. R.(1967) "Inference of Attitudes from Nonverbal Communication in Two Channels". *Journal of Consulting Psychology* 31, 248-252

Mehrabian, Albert, and Wiener, M. (1967) "Decoding of Inconsistent Communications". *Journal of Personality and Social Psychology*. 6, 109-114

Mehrabian, A., and Williams, M. (1969) "Nonverbal Concomitants of Perceived and Intended Persuasiveness". *Journal of Personality and Social Psychology* 1969 13, 37-58

Mehu, Marc, Grammer, Karl, and Dunbar, Robin (Nov 2007) *Evolution and Human Behaviour*. Vol 28, Issue 6 pages 415-422. Oxford University Press

Miller, N. E., Maruyama, G., Beaber, R. J., and Valone, K. (1976) "Speed of Speech and Persuasion". *Journal of Personality and Social Psychology*. 34, 615-624

Packwood, W.T., Meharabian, A., and Williams, M. (1974) "Nonverbal Concomitants of Perceived and Intended Persuasiveness". *Journal of Personality and Social Psychology* 1969 13, 37-58

Prochnow, Herbert, V. (1951) *The Successful Speaker's Handbook*. Prentice-Hall New York

Roth, Charles Byron (1958) *Successful Sales Presentations: How to Build Them*. Prentice-Hall

Rotondo, Jennifer, and Rotondo, Mike Jr.(2002) *Presentation Skills for Managers*. McGraw Hill

Sheehan, Don (1988) *Shut Up and Sell*. AMACOM

Sherman, Bob (June 2002) "10 Presentation Skills Top Executives Live By". In *Business Credit*

Wells, J. C. (2006) *English Intonation: An Introduction*. Cambridge University Press.

Willis, Janine, and Todorov, Alexander (2006) "First Impressions: Making Up Your Mind After a 100-Ms Exposure to a Face". *Psychological Science*: http://webscript.princeton.edu/~tlab/wp-content/publications/Willis&Todorov_PS2006.pdf

Ziglar, Zig (1996) *Zig Ziglar's Secrets of Closing the Sale*. Time Warner International

Index

Lightning Source UK Ltd.
Milton Keynes UK
UKOW05f0645290813

216104UK00001B/14/P